Creative and quirky, yet totally practical. This book is full of brilliant foodie ideas and inspiration. Well done, Steph!

James Wong

ethnobotanist, presenter, garden designer and author

Given that Steph grows such incredible fruit, vegetables and herbs, it's perhaps unsurprising that she would be equally skilled at turning them into incredible food, drinks and more in the kitchen. From creating transforming store cupboard staples to delicious, nutritious lunches and suppers, to healing and refreshing drinks, this book will inspire and enable you to make the best of what's in season.

Mark Diacono

author of award winning books, *A Year at Otter Farm*, *A Taste of the Unexpected* and *The New Kitchen Garden*

Stephanie's book is indispensable for any kitchen, but particularly if you grow your own, as she truly understands harvests and gluts and how you might have to think creatively about what the garden imagines supper might be. There's plenty on storage, teas, cordials and delicious meals year round from what you can grow at home. I promise it will be well thumbed addition.

Alys Fowler

horticulturist, journalist, TV presenter and author

How could everything not be delicious with such beautiful produce fresh from the 'No Dig' garden – just what Stephanie's many devotees have been waiting for.

Darina Allen

award winning author and cookery teacher, Ballymaloe Cookery School

As a disciple of the 'no dig' gardening method that Steph and Charles practice and teach, I am really excited about this new book, *The Creative Kitchen*, from Steph. I have enjoyed many dishes of Steph's cooking at Homeacres so can vouch for these recipes. Don't let 'roasted slugs' or 'spicy rice breakfast soup' put you off. There are tremendous seasonal recipes in here that will do justice to the produce from your vegetable patch or your local farmers' market.

Simon Hill-Norton

co-founder and CEO Sweaty Betty

Steph's fast feasts: I love them and love the looks of wonder when people come in for lunch on course days, greeted by colours, flavours, new ideas; it's all here and more.

Charles Dowding
no dig expert, co-author of *No Dig Organic Home and Gardener*

This wonderful book is an essential reference for anyone who wants to live in a more sustainable way. It is just packed with environmentally friendly, plastic-free ideas covering every aspect of modern living from household cleaners and homemade cosmetics to super-delicious recipes using easy to source ingredients (do try the homemade baked beans). Many of Stephanie's ideas are highly original, some have been around for centuries; Stephanie pulls them all together in one fantastic volume. Established ideas are brought bang up to date and shown to be just as relevant today a they ever were.

We simply can't continue to live in the unsustainable way we currently do; this book can help us all to do our bit and to have fun at the same time. I love it – the world needs this book!

Steve Ott
editor *Kitchen Garden Magazine*

Steph's book is packed full of thrifty, imaginative, colourful and delicious recipes, all test driven by the attendees on her courses. We are in good hands. A lovely book.

Lia Leendertz
garden and cookery writer and author of *The Almanac: a Seasonal Guide*

The Creative Kitchen offers a breath of fresh air to anyone beginning on a journey to a more sustainable lifestyle. Its easy to follow recipes and no nonsense support, shows anyone how they can make their home, along with their diet, a place where earth care and people care really become manageable and simple for everyone to achieve. I would recommend it to anyone with an interest in growing, permaculture and cooking, and applaud Stephanie for creating such a beautiful and yet practical resource. I can't wait to get my copy!

Sara Venn
professional horticulturist and founder of Incredible Edible Bristol

The Creative Kitchen

SEASONAL PLANT BASED RECIPES
FOR MEALS, DRINKS, CRAFTS, BODY & HOME CARE

Stephanie Hafferty

 Permanent Publications

Published by
Permanent Publications
Hyden House Ltd
The Sustainability Centre
East Meon
Hampshire GU32 1HR
United Kingdom
Tel: 01730 823 311
          International code: +44 (0)
Email: enquiries@permaculture.co.uk
Web: www.permanentpublications.co.uk

Distributed in the USA by
Chelsea Green Publishing Company, PO Box 428, White River Junction, VT 05001
www.chelseagreen. com

© 2018 Stephanie Hafferty
The right of Stephanie Hafferty to be identified as the author of this work has been asserted by her in accordance with the Copyrights, Designs and Patents Act 1998

Principal photography by Stephanie Hafferty, additional images:
Heather Edwards: Front cover: main photo, left, right. Back cover: left. Pages 32, 66, 103
Charles Dowding: pages vii, 1, 36, 43, 117, 123
One of Steph's children: pages 52

Designed by Two Plus George Limited, info@twoplusgeorge.co.uk

Printed in the UK by Bell & Bain, Thornliebank, Glasgow

All paper from FSC certified mixed sources.
The Forest Stewardship Council (FSC) is a non-profit international organisation established to promote the responsible management of the world's forests. Products carrying the FSC label are independently certified to assure consumers that they come from forests that are managed to meet the social, economic and ecological needs of present and future generations.

British Library Cataloguing-in-Publication Data
A catalogue record for this book is available from the British Library

ISBN 978 1 85623 323 1

Disclaimer
The information in this book has been compiled for general guidance and is not intended to replace the advice and treatments of qualified herbal practitioners or trained health professionals. Do not attempt to self-diagnose or self-prescribe for serious long-term problems. Heed the cautions given and if pregnant or already taking prescribed medication, seek professional advice before using any herbal remedies or cleaning preparations included in this book.

    If you use any of the information given in this book or recommend it to others, the author and the publisher assume no responsibility for your actions.

    So far as the author and publisher are aware the information is correct and up to date at the time of publishing.

CONTENTS

About the author

Stephanie Hafferty is an award winning author, organic no dig kitchen gardener, writer, blogger and chef, specialising in seasonal plant based food. She is passionate about sharing her knowledge of growing and cooking to feed families and communities. Stephanie regularly writes for *Permaculture Magazine* and other publications, gives talks, workshops and courses on food growing, seasonal cooking and making potions for the home and garden. Stephanie lives as self sufficiently as possible, smallscale homesteading, growing on her allotment and in her smallish garden at her ex-council home.

For my children, Caitlin, Ruairi and Theo

INTRODUCTION: "LOVE ON A PLATE"

I love food! It is absolutely brilliant that something we need to do every day can be so exciting and pleasurable. Food evokes powerful memories: Family meals at my grandma's in Bradford with all of us, somehow, fitting around a dining table which miraculously folded out on Christmas morning; discovering extraordinary new flavours on holidays; and trying to pinch the veg from my sister's plate at dinner time! Growing up, my mum cooked delicious meals from scratch, instilling a love of really flavoursome vegetables at a time when all too often veg was boiled into a tasteless mush. As a teenager, recipe books revealed a new range of culinary possibilities, opening up new flavour sensations. I learnt how to travel the world in the kitchen.

My great grandad had an allotment and my grandad grew strawberries in his back garden, so I grew up knowing about the connection between the soil and what we ate, but it wasn't until my teens that I started to try growing some of my own food and discovered the possibilities of growing and foraging ingredients for wine! As a student in Bristol, I grew a few edible plants on the windowsills of rented rooms. Motherhood and my first productive food garden happened at around the same time; a combined journey of learning how to grow and nurture healthy plants and children. For over a decade, I have been working as a grower in market gardens and running kitchen gardens.

Most of my cooking has been at home, for family and friends. Six years ago I started working as a cook, creating seasonal meals using ingredients almost entirely homegrown by Charles Dowding or myself for our gardening courses at Homeacres. Preparing 10-14 different dishes in a morning, with soup as well during the cooler months, is very exciting: The menu is not planned, it is the freshly harvested provisions brought into the kitchen that morning which decide what the day's menu will be.

Working with edible plants inspires me to try different herb, fruit and vegetable combinations, often nibbling straight from the plant, and creates a strong connection with what is available, fresh and delicious through the seasons. From sowing to caring for the plants and later harvesting, I am thinking about different ways of preparing the food.

This book explains how to turn plant based ingredients into a feast for the senses, using seasonal ingredients you can grow or buy to create meals that make you feel full, nourished and happy. There are meals for special occasions, for sharing, and to make into packed lunches for eating at work or in nature. The recipes are easy to make and use wholesome, seasonal ingredients; good for your health and naturally economical to make.

This book is for everyone, whether you have a productive allotment, a few pots of herbs on the windowsill or buy most of your food ingredients.

The seasonal recipes help you to live lightly, reduce waste and enable a deeper connection with the natural world and rhythm of the seasons, whatever your circumstances. I hope they will inspire you to experiment and try out different flavour combinations of your own.

Almost everything in this book can be grown at home, but not everyone has any space to grow, especially in cities, so everything can easily be bought from local markets or the shops. They are ideal for people who wonder what to do with the ingredients in their veg box, or with a bag full of discounted veg from the bargain shelves at the supermarket. I include recipes for making your own vinegars, sauces and stocks, but it is absolutely fine to use a store bought stock cube instead. The recipes use a lot of beans and peas because these can easily be grown here, but do feel free to replace them with whatever protein you enjoy yourself. These are real life recipes!

I love the colours of these dishes and hope you will too. It's amazing how beautiful plant based food is. After piling her plate high with a selection of salads, one of our course participants looked at her food and said:

"This is love on a plate."

1

STORE CUPBOARD BASICS

Having everything you need in the kitchen makes food preparation so much easier and creating dishes more of a pleasure. Storage is a bit of an issue in my kitchen so I make use of every space possible – including the under stairs cupboard and dresser in my living room!

Here are some of the key items of kitchen equipment and ingredients to have in the cupboard, along with lots of recipes for delicious ingredients to make yourself and use in the recipes in this book, and of course in your own creations.

I have also included some homemade sprays and washes to help wash your homegrown and shop bought produce.

USEFUL KITCHEN EQUIPMENT

It is so tempting to buy every 'time saving' gadget, but these often end up languishing in the back of the cupboard. My kitchen is quite small, so everything needs to have as many uses as possible.

As well as the basics (pots and pans, bowls, wooden spoons, spatula, colander, sieve etc.) the following are very useful.

- **Good knives and a sharpener**
  One large knife and one small, plus a bread knife.

- **Kitchen scissors**
  I find it so useful to have a pair of scissors dedicated to culinary use; ideal for quickly chopping up herbs, dried tomatoes, etc. and also for getting into packets. They live with my knives and – so far – haven't disappeared along with the other pairs of scissors into my boys' rooms.

- **Chopping boards**
  I prefer wood.

- **American cup measures**
  These are invaluable, very quick to use. Try to find the cups which have 1 cup = 236ml, often rounded up to 240ml (true American cups).
  Many in the UK have the larger cup as 250ml, which is the size for Australia, Canada and South Africa. It should be fine to use the larger cups in these recipes, the proportions will be about the same, you will just make a little more.

- **Tablespoon, teaspoon measures**
  These usually come in sets of 4: 1 tbsp, 1 tsp, ½ tsp, ¼ tsp.

- **Weighing scales**
  Digital are the most useful as they can be reset, so you can put a mixing bowl on, set it to zero and then weigh. They are much smaller than the lovely old fashioned scales with weights.

- **An immersion blender**
  Useful for soups, sauces and other smooth liquids; mine has a small food processor too, which can grind or blend small quantities.

- **Food processor**
  Useful for quickly grating all kinds of produce, making hummus, pureés, etc. On a course day when I am often preparing a dozen or more dishes, this is my most used kitchen item (after a knife and chopping board).

- **Pestle and mortar**
  A large one is the most useful; fantastic for grinding spices, nuts and seeds and mixing some salads.

- **Grater or mandolin**
  Ideal for quick food preparation and of course they require no electricity. A four sided box grater is ideal. Do be very careful with fingers!

- **Microplane**
  For fine grating and zesting citrus fruit.

- **Vegetable peeler and julienne**
  Mine are stainless steel; useful for quickly making salads with less washing up.

- **Jars and bottles**
  For storing your ingredients in, your home-made preparations and leftovers in the fridge.

- **A stack of cloths**
  I use white tea towels and old t-shirts. These are fantastic for draining and vegetable drying, and any jobs that one would use paper kitchen towels for, without the waste. (I have white tea towels so I know they are all my paper towel replacements, rather than for drying the dishes.)

USEFUL STORE CUPBOARD INGREDIENTS

Cupboards stocked with the basics make it a lot easier to create meals quickly. Here are some of the key ingredients I always like to have to hand in my kitchen. These are all widely available, even on my small high street here in Bruton, Somerset. International stores are an excellent resource for a wide range of herbs, spices, vinegars and oils, often available to buy in reasonable quantities and usually a lot cheaper than supermarkets.

There are recipes in this book (and in *No Dig Organic Home and Garden*) for infused and flavoured salts, vinegars, sugars, oils, etc.

- **Oils**
  Extra virgin olive, regular olive, extra virgin raw coconut, sunflower, walnut, unrefined sesame.

- **Vinegars**
  Balsamic, wine vinegar (red, white, champagne), rice, apple cider, golden malt (the best for chips), white and brown malt for cooking and making cleaning products.

- **Salts**
  A good sea salt; I also have various kinds of salts from pink to grey, interesting and delicious but not necessary.

- **Black pepper corns**

- **Soy sauce and tamari**

- **Wine**
  Red and white: good quality, organic and/or sulphite free if you can.

- **Dried spices, herbs, edible flowers**

- **Dried tomatoes**

- **Sugar**
  Unbleached granulated, light and dark soft brown.

- **Other sweeteners**
  Maple syrup, agave syrup, vanilla extract (see page 17 for recipe), date molasses, pomegranate molasses.

- **Pulses**
  Homegrown pulses including czar and borlotti, carlin peas, chickpeas, lentils.

- **Nuts and seeds**
  Cashews, sunflower, sesame, hazelnuts, peanuts, pumpkin, walnuts, almonds, flaked coconut.

- **Dried fruit**
  Sultanas, raisins, dates, apricots, prunes.

- **Flour**
  Chickpea (gram/besan/garbanzo), green and yellow pea flour.

- **Oats**

- **Grains**
  Pasta (all kinds), noodles, couscous, barley, rice (brown, wild, white, shortgrain/risotto), quinoa.

- **Tins**
  Life isn't perfect and some tins of basics are extremely useful – tomatoes, chickpeas, borlotti beans, butter beans, mixed beans.

- **Spirits**
  For infusing: vodka, gin, whiskey, brandy, rum or bourbon.

- **Bicarbonate of soda**
  For making some of the potion recipes.

HOMEMADE PRODUCE SPRAYS AND WASHES

To remove insects

They say that the only thing worse than finding a caterpillar in your dinner is finding half a caterpillar! Aphids, caterpillars, slugs and other bugs can find their way into homegrown produce and onto our plates, even after rinsing. Soaking more insect prone harvests for a while before eating helps to remove unwanted creepy crawlies. (If you wish to rescue caterpillars and slugs, remove them as they float to the surface.)

Vegetable soak

This is especially good for salad leaves, leafy greens, cabbages, broccoli and other brassicas.

Fill a large bowl or the kitchen sink with cold water and add:

2 tbsp salt (any kind)

236ml (8fl.oz/1 cup) light vinegar

TIP If you are storing your produce after cleaning, make sure it is dry before doing so – I use clean tea towels.

I usually use cider vinegar, white malt or white wine vinegar is good too. 'Chip shop' brown malt vinegar works but can be a little strong flavoured.

Stir until the salt is dissolved and add the vegetables. Soak for 5-10 minutes, swishing occasionally to make sure the insects are dislodged.

Put the veg into a colander and drain the sink or bowl. Rinse the vegetables under running water to remove the last few aphids and any vinegar solution.

To remove insects from berries

You can use the wash above, but some berries can quickly take on the flavour of the soaking water so instead I use:

1 bowl water

118ml (4fl.oz/½ cup) lemon juice

2 tbsp salt

Soak and rinse as above.

produce spray and wash ingredients

Sprays and washes for cleaning vegetables

These solutions are great for cleaning store bought vegetables that can have oily, waxy residues on the skin.

Produce wash

A large bowl (or the sink) full of cold water plus

236ml (8fl.oz/1 cup) vinegar or

236ml (8fl.oz/1 cup) bicarbonate of soda

Add the produce and soak for an hour. A light tray or similar can be helpful for keeping the produce submerged.

Scrub using a vegetable brush and rinse well under cold water.

Produce spray

1 tbsp lemon juice

1 tbsp bicarbonate of soda

236ml (8fl.oz/1 cup) of water
or
236ml (8fl.oz/1 cup) vinegar

236ml (8fl.oz/1 cup) water

Mix everything together and pour into a spray bottle. Spray your fruit and vegetables, leave for six minutes then scrub with a vegetable brush before rinsing well.

HERB INFUSED SUGARS

Infusing sugar is a delicious way to preserve fresh herbs, saving the distinctive flavours to use year round. These versatile sugars can be used in many ways, replacing regular sugar to add a piquant flavour and interesting twist to: baking, cocktails, fruit salads, on porridge, in hot and cold beverages, in ice cream and sorbets and savoury dishes too that sometimes have sugar as an ingredient – salad dressings, sweet and sour sauces, ketchups. Use your imagination!

Stored for up to a year in glass jars, these sugars are attractive and useful. They make great presents, especially if gifted with some accompanying recipe suggestions. Use single flavour herbs or create your own combinations.

Suggested herbs (use leaves and/or flowers):

Lemon verbena, thyme, lavender, scented geraniums, basil, rosemary, rose, lemon balm, mint, kaffir lime, lemongrass.

Other ingredients that make good sugar infusions: chillies (split), vanilla pods (split), coffee beans, citrus zest, cloves, cinnamon sticks, cardamom pods (lightly crushed).

YOU WILL NEED

5 or 6 sprigs fresh herbs (half the quantity if using dried)

Or 3 tbsp spices/other ingredients (see above)

500g (17½oz/2 cups) sugar

A glass jar with a lid

Shake the herbs to dislodge any insects and dry on a clean kitchen towel. Bruise the herbs gently to release their oils and layer the sugar and herbs in the jar. Replace the lid.

Stir the jar every day for a week. This helps to infuse the sugar and also breaks up any lumping that may occur with the sugar. Then, shake the sugar every day for the following week.

After two weeks of infusing, remove the herbs and compost. Pour the sugar into a clean, labelled jar with a lid. The sugar will keep for about a year.

IDEAS FOR USING INFUSED SUGARS

Mint sugar – delicious in hot chocolate

Lime and chilli – the zest of 1 lime, 2 chillies (split). Use in spicy sauces and to make cocktails.

Elderflower sugar

YOU WILL NEED

Elderflowers

Sugar – I use unbleached organic granulated, but any light coloured sugar is fine

A clean glass jar with a lid

Remove the elderflower blossoms from the stalks with your fingers, they should fall off easily.

Layer sugar and elderflower blossoms alternately in a jar. When full, stir and replace the lid. Leave for two weeks, stirring occasionally to break up any lumps.

This sugar is delicious in baking, as a topping and to fragrantly sweeten beverages.

elderflower and lemon verbena infused sugar

FLAVOURED SALTS

I love to have a selection of infused salts in the kitchen to quickly add depths of flavour to my dishes; just a pinch or two can transform a meal. They are best made using dry, dehydrated ingredients and a good quality salt. Create your own combinations using herbs, vegetables, fruit, edible flowers and spices. You can even make flavoured salts from wine and other drinks.

The flavoured salts make great gifts and last for at least a year.

YOU WILL NEED

Salt – choose a natural, good quality flaked, fine or coarse grain: sea salt, kosher salt, Himalayan, etc.

Dried flavourings – herbs, spices, flowers

A pestle and mortar or electric grinder/ food processor

A dehydrator (optional) to dry ingredients

For each cup of sea salt you will need 4 tsp of ground, dried flavouring

Dehydrate any ingredients that are not already dried (or use the lowest setting on your oven with the door slightly open). The length of time this will take depends on the ingredients you are using; tomatoes will take longer than wild garlic leaves. Refer to your dehydrator's manual for timings. When dry and crisp, blend into a powder in a food processor or grind using a pestle and mortar.

Pour the salt and ground flavouring ingredients into a bowl and mix thoroughly. If you wish to have a finer ground salt, then grind in a pestle and mortar or food processor until the salt granules are your desired size.

Store in a clean glass jar with a label.

wild garlic salt   red wine salt

Wild garlic salt

Gather as many wild garlic leaves as you wish.

Check the wild garlic for any stray weeds and insects. Spread in the dehydrator and dry until crisp. Grind in a food processor until powdered. Pour into a labelled jar. (The dried wild garlic powder will keep for a year and can be used to add flavour to soups, baking, etc.)

Measure 4 tsp wild garlic powder and mix with the salt.

Garlic salt

First of all, make garlic powder. Peel as many cloves of garlic as you wish (and have the space to dehydrate!) and thinly slice. Spread in the dehydrator and dry according to the instructions.

Alternatively, spread on baking trays lined with baking parchment and dry in the oven at the lowest setting until dehydrated. This can take 30–120 minutes, depending on your oven and the thickness of the slices. Check the garlic regularly and turn to ensure thorough drying. When dried and cool, grind into a powder and put into a labelled jar. Use any leftover garlic powder as a seasoning.

Mix 4 tsp garlic powder with the salt.

Rosemary and orange salt

Dehydrate the orange peel and rosemary; grind into a powder.

Rosemary and citrus peel will air dry successfully. Hang bunches of the herb in a cool, airy place to dry (it will take a week or two). Spread the peel on a tray (I use large bamboo herb drying trays) and leave in a cool, airy place to dry.

Mix 2 tsp of ground rosemary and 2 tsp of ground orange peel with the salt.

Scarborough fair salt

Make this delicious mixed herb salt by adding a teaspoon each of dried, ground parsley, sage, rosemary and thyme to the salt.

rosemary and orange salt   Scarborough fair salt

Red wine salt

A deeply flavoured, rich coloured salt, this soon becomes a favourite as an addition to all kinds of meals, marinades, rubs or simply used as a table salt. Just mixing a few spoons full of red wine with salt would not produce much flavour. In this recipe, the wine is simmered so that most of the liquid evaporates, leaving an intensely flavoured syrup.

As with all recipes including alcohol, it is worthwhile using a good quality wine. Experiment with different wines; each will create a different flavoured salt.

I like to use sulphite free if I can.

A 750ml (26fl.oz) bottle of wine

400-550g (14-19oz/1½-2 cups) salt (you may not need all of it)

A baking sheet lined with parchment paper or a clean tea towel (do not use a tea towel if you are drying in the oven)

Or a clean plate and a dehydrator (or line the dehydrator mesh with greaseproof paper)

Pour the wine into a solid, roomy pan and bring to the boil. Reduce the heat and simmer until the liquid has thickened and reduced to about 2 tbsp – this takes about 20-30 minutes. Do keep an eye on it and stir occasionally, especially for the last five minutes or so. Remove from the heat.

Add 1 cup salt and stir until the wine is absorbed. If there is excess wine still in the pan, add another ¼ cup salt and stir. Add another ¼ cup if there is still wine at the bottom of the pan.

Pour onto the baking sheet or plate. Spread out with a fork.

Either:
Leave in an airy place to dry thoroughly, stirring every few hours to prevent sticking,
or
Put in the bottom of the oven on low heat for a few hours, checking occasionally and stirring,
or
Place in the dehydrator on a low setting (150-200ºC, follow your manufacturer's instruction) for an hour or two. Check after the first hour, stir and continue dehydrating if necessary.

When dry, pour into a container and label.

White wine salt is made in the same way. You can also use spirits, for example bourbon or whisky.

BOUILLONS / VEGETABLE STOCK POWDERS

Homemade bouillon powders are a useful addition to the larder, quickly adding depth of flavour to soups, gravies, stews and other dishes. Add a pinch or two to salad dressings, pasta sauces or vegetable juices. Dissolve a ½-1 tsp of powder in a cup of hot water for a quick hot drink (with a pinch of salt to taste).

Homemade stock powder is of course free of unnecessary additives and you can adjust them to suit specific dietary requirements. I like to make mine salt free too, so that I can add salt, or not, according to the dish I am making. It also gives me the opportunity to try out my flavoured salts.

Before processing into a fine powder, I like to store some of the dried vegetables and herbs in a jar to add to meals when I'm very busy and don't have the time for lots of chopping.

Basic bouillon recipe

Vary the ingredients according to the season

2 medium onions

4 garlic cloves (we like garlic, you may prefer 2 or 3 cloves)

3 large carrots

2 stalks celery

1 large leek

1 medium parsnip

1 large potato

3 medium kale leaves, stalks removed (or cabbage, spinach, chard)

2 medium tomatoes

Handful of parsley, including stalks

4 sprigs aromatic herbs – sage, rosemary, thyme

Thinly slice the vegetables and garlic and chop the leaves and herbs into small pieces.

Arrange the vegetables and herbs on the dehydrator, keeping the same kind together so that you can easily remove the faster drying ingredients, leaving the slower drying to continue dehydrating. They take different times to dehydrate due to different water content – parsley will be ready before leeks, for example.

Dehydrate according to the directions on your machine. When everything has dried, leave to cool.

Put in a food processor or blender, add any extras you want – sea salt, black pepper, dried chilli, other dried herbs or spices such as dried turmeric or ginger – and blitz. You may need to do this in several batches. If so, for each batch, place into a large bowl and mix with a spoon when it is all done.

Store in labelled glass jars in a cool, dry, dark cupboard.

Wild herb bouillon

A totally wild super green powder, this is a lovely way of preserving wild plants, especially for the winter months. Rinse and dry the herbs before using.

Gather a handful each of four or more seasonal wild herbs e.g. wild garlic, nettles, chickweed, garlic mustard, dandelion, wild fennel, chicory, fat hen, salad burnet, watercress.

Dehydrate, then blend into a powder when dry.

Mushroom bouillon

You can use wild or cultivated mushrooms; the flavour will vary with your choice. Dehydrating mushrooms is a great way to preserve them if they are on offer in shops or markets. If you wish, replace the fresh mushrooms with 50g dried.

500g (17½oz/6 cups) fresh mushrooms, sliced
2 medium onions
4 garlic cloves (we like garlic, you may prefer 2 or 3 cloves)
3 large carrots
2 stalks celery
1 large leek
Handful of parsley, including stalks
4 sprigs aromatic herbs – sage, rosemary, thyme

Slice the mushrooms and spread across the dehydrator trays. Dry according to the manufacturer's instructions.

When dry, blend into a powder.

You can also store some of the mushrooms whole in glass jars to add to your meals.

vegetable bouillon

tomato bouillon

fruit bouillon

Tomato bouillon

As many tomatoes as you wish (or have space for in the dehydrator/oven), any kind.

Slice the tomatoes and deseed. Spread out on the dehydrator racks making sure they do not touch, to ensure even drying.

Dehydrate according to the manufacturer's instructions for five hours, then turn over and continue for another five hours until very dry and crisp.

Allow to cool, then blend into a powder.

Add water to make up your own tomato paste, juice and sauce.

Note: this makes surprisingly little powder for the quantity of tomatoes, but the flavour is amazing!

Fruit bouillon

A delicious way to preserve gluts of fruit, or bargains found in stores, this intensely flavoured bouillon also provides vitamins.

Uses:
- Add water to your bouillon to make a fruity drink
- Sprinkle onto breakfast cereals
- Add to sauces, salad dressings and marinades
- Sprinkle on top of homemade baked goods, sweets (candies) and chocolate truffles
- Add a couple of teaspoons to cake batters and frostings
- Add to gravies for a luxurious flavour
- Mix with salt to make a rub

Any fruit, sliced and peeled/deseeded (if applicable).

Dehydrate the fruit according to your dehydrator's instructions (or use the oven method on page 10), arranging it so that the same fruit is together, if you are dehydrating different kinds.

When totally dry and crisp, process in the blender until powdered.

Either process separately and store as individually flavoured fruits, or combine in the blender.

Store in labelled jars.

TIP If you live in a humid area, freeze the fruit before blending. This also works well for the tomatoes.

STOCK

A good stock forms the basis for soups and many other recipes. I have omitted salt and pepper in these recipes as I add that to the dish itself, but you can add 1 tsp black peppercorns and 1 tsp sea salt to these recipes, if you like.

Add whatever odds and ends of vegetable trimmings and peelings you have, making sure that you do not add darker vegetables such as beetroot or onion skins to the light stock.

They will store in covered jars for three days in the fridge or alternatively freeze.

Light vegetable stock

3 litres (105fl.oz/12½ cups) water

500g (17½oz/4 cups) vegetable odds and ends (replace with more of the other veg if you have no odds and ends)

2 medium parsnips

2 onions, peeled and sliced

4 stalks celery, chopped

4 carrots, chopped

2-4 cloves garlic, peeled and chopped

2 leeks, chopped

1 cup parsley including stems, chopped

1 bay leaf

2 sprigs thyme

A large stock pot or slow cooker

Put the vegetables and water in the pan, the water should be at least 2.5cm/1in above the vegetables so add a little more if necessary and bring to the boil.

Reduce the heat and simmer for two hours. Leave to cool, strain through a sieve (adding the pulp to the compost) and store in the fridge or freeze.

Dark vegetable stock

The ingredients are the same, but add beetroot, dark greens (such as kale) and onion skins.

Preheat the oven to 180°C fan (200°C/400°F/gas mark 6).

Spread the vegetables over two roasting tins, drizzle over olive oil, coating the vegetables with a brush or your fingers.

Roast for 45-60 minutes until cooked and browned at the edges.

Scrape the roasting tins with a wooden spatula to remove all of the oil and brown bits, adding a little water to help get everything off and into the stockpot if needed.

Place the roasted vegetables, herbs and water into the stockpot; the water should be at least 2.5cm/1in above the vegetables so add a little more if necessary and bring to the boil.

Reduce the heat and simmer for two hours. Leave to cool, strain through a sieve (adding the pulp to the compost) and store in the fridge or freeze.

TIP   If you have a woodburner, during the winter months simmer the stock on this after it has been brought to the boil on the cooker. I find this takes about three hours, but is free! During the summer months, I use a slow cooker, which uses less electricity than my cooker.

VANILLA

Vanilla extract

This delicious store cupboard ingredient takes a while to infuse (up to two months) but it is well worth the wait.

I usually use vodka; alternatively use rum, brandy, whisky or bourbon.

YOU WILL NEED

240ml (8fl.oz/1 cup) vodka

4 vanilla beans

A clean lidded jar

A clean bottle to store it in

Split the vanilla beans in half down their length.

Place in the jar and pour over the alcohol, making sure the beans are submerged. Shake and place in a cool, dark place where you will remember it – a cupboard that you open regularly is ideal.

Shake the jar every day for the first month, ensuring that the beans remain submerged.

Taste a little of the vanilla extract. Leave it to infuse for longer if you prefer a stronger flavour; up to two months.

Strain through muslin and store in a clean labelled bottle.

Place the used vanilla pods on a clean tea towel in an airy place and allow to dry. Store in a clean dry jar to use when cooking (to flavour sweet sauces, for example) or make vanilla sugar.

Vanilla sugar

Used vanilla beans*

Sugar – I use unbleached, organic sugar

A clean glass jar

Half fill the jar with sugar. Scrape any seeds remaining in the pods into the sugar and stir. Add the pods and pour over more sugar until the jar is full.

Leave for three weeks to infuse, shaking every few days. For a stronger flavour, leave the beans a little longer.

Remove the pods and label the jar.

You can use those sugary pods one last time to lightly infuse sweet sauces or hot drinks, before composting.

* If you are using fresh vanilla pods scrape all of the seeds into the sugar and stir. Add the pods and leave to infuse. This will take a week or so.

HOMEMADE ALTERNATIVES FOR CITRUS IN A RECIPE

Here in Somerset, I have some small citrus trees but weather conditions here mean that they produce just a few precious fruit each year, so most of my citrus fruit has to be bought and is of course imported.

There are many other recipe ideas for using leftover citrus peels in *No Dig Organic Home and Garden*.

These alternatives are useful to have to hand for the savoury recipes in this book if you do not have any citrus fruit in the kitchen.

Citrus flavoured herbs to grow in your garden or kitchen:
- Lemon balm
- Lemon and lime basil
- Lemon, lime, grapefruit and orange mint
- Lemon verbena
- Lemongrass
- Kaffir lime
- Lemon thyme
- Lemon, lime and citrus scented pelargonium

kaffir lime
infused vinegar

lemongrass
vinegar

Using zest

If I am not using the zest in a recipe, I always remove it with a microplane or zester and either dry or freeze it until needed. It is useful to have three little labelled pots in the freezer for lemon, lime and orange zest.

Replace a tablespoon of citrus juice with ⅓ tbsp zest with ⅔ tbsp water, in recipes.

lemon balm infused
white wine

lemon verbena
infused vodka

Citrus scented herb infused vinegar

Each of these have a different lemony flavour so it is well worth trying them all and choose for yourself which tastes best for different recipes.

Use ½ tsp vinegar for each tsp citrus juice in a recipe.

For all of these you will need a clean lidded jar for infusing and another labelled jar or bottle to store your finished vinegar.

YOU WILL NEED

Fresh herbs (or half the quantity of dried) – lemon verbena, lemon balm, lemon (etc.) basil, lemon (etc.) mint

Light vinegar (cider, white wine, champagne)

Half fill the jar with the fresh herbs (or ¼ fill if using dried) and pour over the vinegar to fill. Leave to infuse, shaking daily, for two weeks. Strain through a sieve and bottle.

Lemon thyme vinegar

2 sprigs lemon thyme

472ml (16fl.oz/2 cups) vinegar – white wine or champagne vinegar is especially good with thyme

Pour the vinegar into the jar and add the sprigs, ensuring they are submerged. Leave to infuse, shaking daily, for two weeks. Strain through a sieve and bottle.

Lemongrass vinegar

3 stalks lemongrass

472ml (16fl.oz/2 cups) vinegar – rice vinegar is especially good or use cider or white wine vinegar

Thinly slice the lemongrass and put in a strong glass jar. Using a wooden spoon or muddler, crush to release the flavours. Pour over the vinegar and shake. Leave to infuse for two days to two weeks (for a stronger flavour).

Strain and bottle.

Kaffir lime infused vinegar

Fresh kaffir lime leaves (or half the quantity of dried)

Light vinegar (cider, white wine, champagne)

Tear the leaves into quarters and crush gently. Half fill the jar with leaves and pour over the vinegar to fill. Leave to infuse, shaking daily, for two weeks. Strain through a sieve and bottle.

Lemon balm infused white wine

This delicious infused wine can be used in place of lemon juice in a recipe and also tastes gorgeous as an aperitif. I always let some coriander go to seed so that I can harvest the zingy green seeds. They are delicious sprinkled onto salads and hummus too.

In a recipe, it can be used 1:1 with lemon juice (so if the recipe asks for 1 tbsp juice, use 1 tbsp infused wine).

236ml (8fl.oz/1 cup) white wine (⅓ bottle)

12 lemon balm leaves

1 tsp green coriander seeds (if you have them) or ½ tsp dried

Tear the leaves and put into a strong glass jar. Using a wooden spoon, gently bruise. Add the coriander seeds and wine. Replace the lid, shake and leave in a cool place overnight.

Strain and bottle. It will keep in the fridge for about a week.

Lemon verbena infused vodka

Try making this with the other citrus flavoured herbs too. It makes a delicious base for cocktails as well as salad dressings and like the vanilla extract recipe, could also be used in baking. This vodka is an attractive light green and makes a lovely gift.

Vodka

Lemon verbena (or other leafy herb) leaves

Half fill the jar with leaves and gently crush with a wooden spoon to release the oils. Fill the jar with vodka and leave to infuse in a dark, dry cupboard which is regularly opened, so that you will remember to shake it every day for a month.

Strain, bottle and label. This will keep for at least a year.

Herb infused simple syrup

This sweet flavoured syrup lends itself to salad dressings, desserts and baking; it also tastes delicious as a hot drink, or with sparkling water, or as an ingredient in cocktails.

250g (8oz/1 cup) sugar

250g (8oz/1 cup) water

Herbs:
6 sprigs basil, thyme, mint, lemon verbena or pelargonium including flowers if in season,
or
12 leaves kaffir lime,
or
3 stalks lemongrass, lightly crushed

Combine the sugar and water in a saucepan and bring to the boil. Stir until the sugar dissolves, remove from the heat and add the herbs.

Leave to cool for two hours.

Strain through a fine sieve and bottle. This will keep in the fridge for two weeks.

TIP You can use other herbs (for example rosemary, thyme, basil), edible flowers (such as elderflowers, basil flowers or roses), spices and citrus peels to make simple syrups in the same way. Add dried fruit bouillon powder (page 14) for a quick fruit cordial.

HERB AND SPICE MIXES

I find it useful to have some dried herb and spice mixes ready made up in jars on my shelf. These are some of my favourite blends.

Za'atar style

Traditionally Za'atar contains sumac. Add 4 tsp ground sumac to this recipe for a more authentic flavour.

2 tsp thyme

2 tsp oregano

4 tsp cumin

4 tsp toasted sesame seeds

1 tsp sea salt

Grind in a pestle and mortar or blender until fine.

Toasted cumin, fennel and coriander seed

This is my go-to for hummus and many salad dressings.

4 tsp cumin seed

4 tsp fennel seed

4 tsp coriander seed

Dry roast the seeds, cool and grind into a fine powder.

Ras el hanout style

Lovely sprinkled onto roasted vegetables.

1 tsp cumin seeds

1 tsp ground ginger

1 tsp coriander seeds

1 tsp ground nutmeg

1 tsp turmeric

1 tsp fennel seeds

2 tsp cinnamon or 1 cinnamon stick, ground

1 tsp smoked paprika or red pepper flakes

1 tsp black pepper

1 tsp cayenne
(optional – if you like it spicy!)

5 star anise

½ tsp ground cloves

Seeds from 10 cardamom pods

1 tsp dried rose petals

Dry roast the cumin, coriander, peppercorns, fennel and star anise. Cool and mix with the other ingredients in a pestle and mortar or blender until finely ground.

Pour through a fine sieve to remove any bits before storing.

TIP To dry roast seeds or spices, pour into a hot pan and stir for two minutes until fragrant.

mixed cumin, fennel and coriander seed

Herbes de Provence

2 tsp thyme

2 tsp rosemary

2 tsp oregano (or marjoram)

2 tsp mint

2 tsp basil

2 tsp summer savory

1 tsp fennel seeds

1 tsp lavender flowers

Grind in a pestle and mortar or blender until fine.

Fine herbes

I love French tarragon, it is such a flavoursome and versatile herb. *Fine Herbes* is a great way of storing the flavour in the autumn, for winter use.

1 tbsp French tarragon

1 tbsp chives

1 tbsp chervil

1 tbsp parsley

2 tsp thyme

Chop all of the herbs and mix together.

This is also delicious made with fresh herbs, using the same ratios.

FIVE OIL FREE SALAD DRESSINGS

For an oil free option, replace the salad dressings in the recipes with these. The tahini salad dressing on page 61 is also oil free.

Cashew and orange salad dressing

130g (4½oz/1 cup) cashews, soaked for 2 hours and drained

236ml (8fl.oz/1 cup) orange juice (2-4 oranges, depending on size and juiciness)

2 oranges, zest

2 tsp fresh seasonal herbs, chopped (basil, chervil, parsley, dill)

3 tbsp sunflower seeds, soaked for 2 hours and drained

Salt and pepper to taste (optional)

Reserve the nut and seed soaking liquid.

Put all of the ingredients in a food processor and blend, adding some of the soaking liquid until the dressing is the thickness you wish.

Season with salt and pepper and stir.

Lemon vinaigrette

118ml (4fl.oz/½ cup) lemon juice

1 lemon, finely chopped zest

8 tbsp water

1-2 cloves garlic, minced

1 tbsp dijon or wholegrain mustard

2 tbsp lemon balm or mint, finely chopped (or parsley/chervil in the winter)

Salt and pepper to taste (optional)

Place all of the ingredients in a jug and whisk. Taste and add more water if it is too sharp.

Summer fruit vinaigrette

150g (5¼oz/1 cup) sweet seasonal summer fruits (strawberries, raspberries, blueberries etc.)

1 tbsp vinegar – cider or red wine

1 tbsp water

Salt and pepper to taste (optional)

Place the ingredients in a food processor and blend into a smooth dressing.

TIP If you want to use tarter fruits (e.g. redcurrants, blackcurrants) add 1-2 tbsp agave or maple syrup to sweeten to your taste.

Tamari and lime salad dressing

3 tbsp tamari

1 tbsp lime juice

½ tsp ginger, minced

1-3 garlic cloves, minced

¼ cup water

Salt and pepper to taste (optional)

Whisk together and serve.

Czar bean salad dressing

160g (5½oz/1 cup) cooked czar beans (⅔ of a can of drained beans)

236ml (8fl.oz/1 cup) water or the bean cooking liquid (you may need a little more)

2 tbsp tahini (oil free)

1 tbsp dijon mustard

1 tbsp lemon juice

2 tbsp seasonal herbs, chopped (e.g. dill, parsley, coriander, French tarragon, thyme)

Salt and pepper to taste (optional)

Place all of the ingredients with ½ cup of the water in a food processor and blend. Slowly add more liquid until the dressing is the consistency you desire.

INFUSED OILS AND VINEGARS

I share many recipes for infused oils and vinegars in *No Dig Organic Home and Garden*. Easy to make, you can use them to add your own unique flavours to sweet and savoury dishes including dressings, sauces and soups, and many can form the base for homemade home and skin preparations, including those in Chapter 6. They also make beautiful gifts.

Here are some other recipes for you to try.

Elderflower vinegar

This delicious vinegar can be used to make salad dressings, as a cordial (with something sweet added: sugar, agave, maple syrup, honey) and in homemade cosmetics including hair rinses and skin splashes.

12 heads elderflowers

500ml (17fl.oz/2 cups) white wine or champagne vinegar

Simply put the elderflowers and vinegar in a jar, replace the lid and shake. Allow the vinegar to infuse for two weeks, shaking daily, then strain through a sieve lined with muslin or a jelly bag and pour into a clean, labelled bottle.

You can use cider vinegar if you prefer. To make a skin toner, use the same method but replace the vinegar with witch hazel.

The vinegar will keep for up to a year.

Fruit balsamic vinegar

Rich, sweet and fruity, this is delicious as a cordial and makes a fabulous glaze for roasted vegetables. Replace the balsamic with red or white wine or cider vinegar, as you wish. It's a great way of quickly preserving a summer fruit glut.

1kg (35oz/8 cups) soft fruit (blackcurrants, blackberries, raspberries, strawberries, etc.)

600ml (21fl.oz/2½ cups) balsamic vinegar

700g (24oz/3½ cups) unbleached granulated sugar (approximately, see recipe)

A large glass jar with a noncorrosive lid

Bottles or jars for storing with noncorrosive lids

Optional extras – spices or herbs: 1 cinnamon stick, piece of ginger the size of your thumb, sliced, ½ tsp cloves, 2-3 sprigs of rosemary, thyme or lemon verbena

Clean the fruit and check for stalks and insects. Dry with a clean cloth and pour into the jar. Mash lightly with a potato masher or muddler. Add spices or herbs if using.

Pour the vinegar into the jar, stir and seal. Place in a cool, dark cupboard for a week, shaking every day.

Strain into a large container through a muslin lined sieve or jelly bag. Cover with a clean damp tea towel (to stop flies visiting) and leave the fruit to drip overnight.

The next day, prepare your clean bottles for the hot liquid by putting them in a low oven 130°C (275°F/gas mark ½) making sure they are not touching (this also sterilises them). Remove the lids and place on the rack separately, after making sure that they are ovenproof. If you are using lids with a plastic coating on the inside, put these in a bowl of boiling water. Leave the jars in the oven for 30 minutes. Use tongs and oven gloves to remove when you're ready to fill them.

Measure the fruit vinegar into a large pan. For each 500ml (17fl.oz/2 cups) liquid, add 400g (14oz/2 cups) sugar and bring to the boil. Reduce the heat to a gentle boil and cook for 10 minutes.

Carefully pour using a funnel into the hot jars. Wipe the tops with a damp cloth before sealing and place on a wooden board or table to cool.

Label when cool. The vinegar is ready immediately and will store in a cool place for up to a year. Keep in the fridge once opened.

Herb infused olive oil

This is a quick method, using a bain marie.

To make infused oils, always use clean, dry herbs and discard any which have signs of mould or disease. It's important to make sure the herbs are dry, so spread out on a clean cloth for a few hours to make sure any traces of moisture have gone.

**SUGGESTED QUANTITIES FOR
250ml (8fl.oz/1 cup) OLIVE OIL**

4 sprigs rosemary

4 sprigs thyme

4 springs lemon verbena

Basil, parsley, coriander, shiso, marjoram and other leafy herbs, about ½ the quantity of herbs to oil (ratio 2 parts oil to 1 part herbs)

Place the herbs and oil in the bain marie, bring the water to the boil then reduce to a low simmer and slowly warm the oil for an hour.

Remove from the heat and allow to cool before straining through a sieve lined with muslin. Compost the herbs.

Using a funnel, carefully pour the oil into clean, sterilised jars. Seal and label.

For culinary use, keep refrigerated and use within a month. If you are using the oil to make body potions, use within six months or up to a year for household cleaners etc. Always discard any oil which looks or smells bad.

Elderflower oil

1 part elderflowers

3 parts oil
(I use half olive and half grapeseed)

Place your elderflowers in a jar. Fill with approximately three times as much oil. It doesn't have to be exact, but if you prefer, weigh the elderflowers and measure out three times that quantity of oil.

Stir and place something on top to help keep the elderflowers submerged, such as a plastic canning lid.

Leave in a cool, dark place for two weeks. Strain through a muslin lined sieve and pour into a clean labelled jar.

Keep refrigerated and use within a month in the kitchen, or within six months for non-culinary preparations.

I mainly make it to use in soaps, salves and other body products. Elderflower oil is soothing, anti-inflammatory and kind to the skin.

HOW TO MAKE YOUR OWN VINEGAR

Making vinegar is a fun, thrifty way of transforming leftover wine and other alcoholic drinks into a delicious, useful condiment. Mix those odds and ends of wine left in bottles at the end of a party together (I prefer to keep red and white separate), add the mother (see below) and a few months later, enjoy your fragrant homemade vinegar.

You can also create your own specific brews, such as Merlot Vinegar or Prosecco Vinegar.

Traditionally, vinegar is made in wooden barrels or earthenware pots with a spigot at the bottom for removing the vinegar. You can improvise with what you already have at home, large preserving jars are ideal, or search charity shops for Rumtopf, flour or other large pottery containers.

Ensure that everything is sparkling clean before making the vinegar.

Homemade wine vinegar

YOU WILL NEED

Red or white wine

A vinegar 'mother'

Glass or ceramic container with a wide mouth

Muslin or cheesecloth to cover

Muslin, cheesecloth or coffee filters

Elastic band for fastening

Clean bottles or jars for storing, with labels

TIP I use water that has been filtered by my Berkey carbon filters, alternatively use cooled boiled spring or tap water (leave tap water uncovered for 24 hours to remove as much chlorine as possible).

The mother is a slimy rubbery substance made from acetic acid bacteria and cellulose. I use a mother from apple cider vinegar. It came from a friend and it's worth asking around to see if someone has a spare mother they could donate (online forums are useful for this purpose). Alternatively, health food shops usually have several varieties of raw unpasteurised apple cider vinegar with the mother. Strain the vinegar through muslin or a coffee filter to extract the mother.

Pour the wine into the container, to about half full. Cover with muslin and fasten with an elastic band, to prevent dust or insects falling in and leave overnight.

The next day, add the mother and replace the muslin cover. Place the jar in a cool, dark place such as a kitchen cupboard. Depending on the wine and the time of year, it can take from two weeks to two months for fermentation to start properly (longer in the winter, faster in warmer summer months).

As the brew ferments, it will go through a pretty smelly phase before the wine is transformed into a sour vinegar. Stir regularly and taste. If you see a film on the surface, that is just the mother. Submerge it and replace to continue fermenting.

You can add a glass or two of spare wine during this process, however do not fill the container more than ⅔ full.

It can take up to six months for the vinegar to be ready so do not worry if your brew is taking a long time. During this time, as the mother grows and thickens, remove some and use it to make another batch of vinegar or share with friends.

When the vinegar is ready, filter three or four times through a muslin lined sieve to make sure that all particles are removed as much as possible and store in clean, labelled bottles.

Use the youngest mother to start your next batch (it will have been floating nearest to the surface) and discard an old mother reclining at the bottom of the vessel. I compost mine.

Use the same method to make other alcohol based vinegars.

Champagne vinegar

It's not often that there is leftover champagne, but you can also use prosecco and other sparkling wines.

For each 500ml (17fl.oz/2 cups) champagne, add 250ml (8½fl.oz/ 1 cup) water. Continue as for wine vinegar.

Sherry vinegar

For each 250ml (8½fl.oz/1 cup) sherry, add 500ml (17fl.oz/2 cups) water. Continue as for wine vinegar.

Homebrew wine vinegar

Use your home brews in the same way as wine vinegar.

Beer/malt vinegar

Beer, ale and lager can be made into vinegar in the same way as wine vinegar.

Apple cider vinegar

In the UK, apple cider is a fermented alcoholic drink but in the US this is known as hard cider (apple cider being a non alcoholic beverage). Make in the same way as wine vinegar.

You can use apple juice/non alcoholic versions of cider in this way but it will take a lot longer.

malt vinegar
with the mother

Vinegar from fruit scraps

A thrifty way of using up scraps of apples or pears which would otherwise have been composted. Use peelings, cores and other discarded parts of the fruit.

Sugar water – enough to cover the scraps; for each 1 litre (34fl.oz/4 cups) water add 50g (1½oz /¼ cup) sugar

Fruit scraps

Several preserving jars (or one large one)

Muslin to cover

Elastic band to fasten

Make the sugar water: bring the water to the boil in a pan, add the sugar and stir until dissolved. Set aside to cool.

Chop the scraps and place in the jars to about ¾ full. Pour over the sugar syrup ensuring that all of the scraps are submerged in the liquid, cover with the muslin and set aside at room temperature.

After about a week, the brew should be bubbling and turning a dark colour. When the bubbling stops, strain, compost the scraps and continue as for wine vinegar.

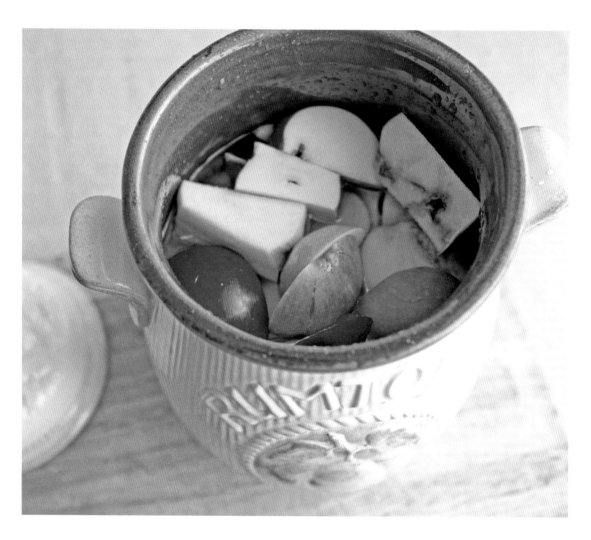

2

SOUP

Just the thought of a bowl of homemade soup can make a person feel warm inside! All of the goodness of the vegetables, herbs and spices fuse together in the soup pan, nurturing and nourishing. Wholesomely thrifty, soup can hide all kinds of wonky vegetables and use up odds and ends in the kitchen. I like to make a large pan of soup to last for several days, storing it in glass jars in the fridge. It feels reassuring knowing that it is there, a quick tasty warming meal in moments. Serve with fresh bread and seasonal salad leaves or sprouts.

Hearty bean and vegetable soup

This soup is delicious with any homegrown dried beans, or use tinned beans for a quick, filling meal.

This recipe makes plenty of soup for four people, including seconds, and keeps well in the fridge for two or three days.

SERVES 4

240g (8½oz/1½ cups) cooked beans

135g (4½oz/1 cup) onions, chopped

120g (4oz/1 cup) leeks, sliced (1 leek)

2-4 cloves garlic

170g (6oz/1½ cups) celery (2 stalks)

500g (17½oz/3½ cups) vegetables, diced – parsnip, beetroot, squash, carrot, potato, celeriac etc.

50g (1½oz/1 cup) kale, spinach or other green leaves, shredded

1 tbsp fresh parsley, chopped

1 tsp fresh thyme, chopped

A little olive oil for frying

1½ litres (50fl.oz/6½ cups) vegetable stock or water

Salt and pepper to taste

Drizzle some oil into a large pan on the stove, add the onions, leeks, garlic and celery and cook on a low heat, stirring occasionally, until soft.

Add the rest of the vegetables, herbs, beans and stock or water and bring to the boil. Then turn the heat down for 20-30 minutes until the vegetables are cooked through.

Remove 450ml (16fl.oz/2 cups) of the soup, put into a large jug and blend with an immersion blender. (This step is optional, it makes the soup creamier and thicker.)

Return the puréed vegetables to the soup pan, stir thoroughly and season to taste.

Serve with crusty bread and a green salad.

Vegetable market,
Luang Prabang, Laos

Spicy rice breakfast soup

This recipe is based on the delicious breakfast soups I have eaten in Thailand and Laos. There, the soups are very spicy which certainly wakes you up! I love soup for breakfast, but this soup is equally delicious at any time of the day.

This is moderately spicy. Adjust the garlic, chilli and ginger to suit your tastebuds.

1.3 litres (48fl.oz/6 cups) vegetable stock

135g (4½oz/1 cup) onions, chopped (or spring onions, leeks or shallots)

170g (6oz/1½ cups/2 sticks) celery, thinly sliced

1 stalk lemongrass, cut into 1in pieces and gently crushed (if you don't have any lemongrass, leave it out or add some sprigs of lemon verbena or lemon balm)

360g (12½oz/2 cups) brown rice, cooked

2 tbsp tamari or other soy sauce

125g (4oz/1 cup) seasonal vegetables, chopped (e.g. kale, spinach, broccoli, sweet pepper, chard)

1 tbsp lime juice

2in piece of fresh ginger, peeled

1-3 chillies

2-4 garlic cloves

3 tbsp coriander roots and stems

Fresh coriander or parsley

A little oil for cooking (olive, sunflower, rapeseed, coconut)

130g (4½oz/1 cup) cashew nuts or cooked beans (optional) if you want a more substantial soup

A large soup pan

Chop the chillies, garlic, coriander roots and stems and ginger and put into a pestle and mortar. Pound gently into a paste. (If you don't have a pestle and mortar, finely chop everything or blend in a food processor.)

Drizzle some oil into the pan and add the chopped onions and celery. Cook on a low heat until the onions are transparent, add the chilli mixture and lemongrass* and stir.

Add the vegetables, stock, tamari, cashews or beans (if using) and rice. Bring to the boil, reduce heat and simmer for 20 minutes. Add the lime juice and stir.

Pour into bowls and sprinkle with fresh chopped coriander or parsley.

* The lemongrass is for flavour, not to eat. I just remove it from my bowl as I'm eating, but if you prefer, remove it from the pan with a slotted spoon before serving.

TIP Replace 1 cup of the stock with coconut milk for a creamier soup.

TIP If you accidentally make this too spicy for your taste, add a can of coconut milk.

Divine beetroot soup

A deep sensual red with flavours to match, this soup looks and tastes special. It's a good way of using up beetroot that has gone a little soft in storage. I have also used leftover Beetroot Salad (see pages 62-64) and frozen beetroot in this too.

I used red beetroot here: yellow beetroot changes the colour and flavour a little but is still very delicious.

Protect your clothes while making this, especially when blending the soup – it stains and takes some cleaning if you accidentally shoot it up the wall (I have done this!).

1kg (35oz/7 cups) beetroot, peeled and diced (or equal quantities of beetroot and carrots)

1 litre (35fl.oz/4¼ cups) stock

270g (9½oz/2 cups) onions, finely chopped

2 garlic cloves

1-2 chillies, chopped (optional)

1-2 tbsp ginger (according to taste)

2 tsp coriander, cumin and fennel seed blend (see page 22)

3 oranges, juice and finely chopped zest

2 tbsp olive or other light oil

Salt and pepper to taste

Fresh coriander, chervil or parsley to garnish

Pour the oil into a large soup pan and add the onions, garlic, ginger and chilli (if using). Cook over a low heat until the onions are softened. Add the spice mix, beetroot, zest, orange juice and stock, bring to the boil, reduce heat and simmer for around 45 minutes until the vegetables are soft.

Remove from the heat and carefully(!), purée using an immersion blender. If you'd prefer not to, it is absolutely fine to serve the soup like this, with tasty beetroot chunks.

Pour into bowls and garnish with freshly chopped herbs and vegetable crisps. Serve with crusty bread.

The soup tastes lovely without the oranges, if you do not have any. Just add a little extra stock when cooking.

Velvety roasted squash soup

This soup tastes especially good using one of the sweet, nutty full flavoured squashes: e.g. Uchiki Kuri, Crown Prince, Marina di Chioggia, however you can use any squash or pumpkin that you have. When using a less flavoursome squash, I usually replace 400ml of the stock with coconut milk for extra richness.

You can replace the squash with diced summer squash, courgettes or marrows.

Roasting the squash first really brings out the flavour, but if you don't have the time then simply adding raw diced squash to the soup will be fine. I always make full use of the oven and roast extra squash and use it to make salads, curries and other dishes.

Ingredients
1.6kg (56oz/8 cups) squash, peeled and diced (Uchiki Kuri, butternut, summer squash and courgettes do not need peeling)
1 whole head garlic
270g (9½oz/2 cups) onions, finely chopped
100g (3½oz/1 cup) celery, sliced
300g (10½oz/1 cup) carrots, chopped
1-2 chillies (optional)
3cm piece of ginger, peeled and chopped
2 tbsp coriander, roots and stems (or just stems), chopped
1.9kg (67fl.oz/8 cups) vegetable stock
Olive oil
Salt and pepper to taste
Fresh coriander to garnish

Preheat the oven to 180°C fan (200°C/400°F/gas mark 6).

Spread the diced squash on the trays, placing the whole head of garlic on too. Drizzle with olive oil and roast for 20-25 minutes until cooked.

Put on one side to cool a little. Remove the garlic and put on a cool plate – you will be handling this so it needs to be a moderate temperature.

Add 2 tbsp oil to a large soup pan and sauté the onions, carrots, chillies, ginger, garlic and coriander roots/stems on a low heat, stirring occasionally, for 15-20 minutes. This may need a cup of stock if it looks too dry.

Add the squash and then the stock. Squeeze in the soft garlic purée from the roasted head of garlic. Bring to the boil and simmer for 20 minutes.

Add salt and pepper to taste, then purée using an immersion blender.

Serve sprinkled with fresh herbs.

Summery raw tomato and basil soup

This soup makes the most of seasonal tomato abundance and is fantastic for summer packed lunches. Just pour into lidded jars, sprinkle on the topping and you are good to go.

300g (10oz/2 cups) tomatoes, diced

10g (½oz/½ cup) fresh sweet basil

120ml (4fl.oz/½ cup) water or ½ cucumber, chopped

½ lemon, juice

1 garlic clove, finely chopped (optional)

Salt and pepper to taste

Finely chopped tomatoes and basil to garnish

Place all of the soup ingredients in a blender or food processor and combine. Taste and season. It's that simple.

Sprinkle with chopped tomatoes and basil before eating.

TIP Replace 1 or 2 tsp of the sweet basil with mint or one of the stronger flavoured basils (lemon, lime, Thai) to vary the flavours.

Creamy salad soup with sautéed leaves

A delicious way of using up gluts of seasonal leaves, this recipe can use mixed salads or just one kind of lettuce, whatever you have. It will taste different every time you make it, as the varieties of leaves change with the seasons. This soup is tasty chilled too, so is great for packed lunches.

500g (18oz) seasonal leaves (a whole lettuce or mixture of lettuce, chard, kale, spinach, mustards, oriental greens, rocket, etc.)

PLUS

A bunch of leaves for topping (optional)

270g (9½oz/2 cups) onions or leeks, diced

140g (5oz/1 cup) potatoes, diced and peeled

240g (8½oz/1½ cups) peas or broad beans (frozen are fine if that's what you have) or 2 cups cooked beans in the winter

2-3 cloves of garlic, finely chopped, according to taste

2 tbsp fresh parsley or mint, chopped, plus more to decorate

700ml (24½fl.oz/3 cups) stock

4 tbsp olive oil

Salt and pepper to taste

½ lemon, juice (optional)

Put 2 tbsp of oil in the soup pan and add the onions (or leeks) and garlic. Sauté until the onion is soft, then add the chopped leaves and stir. Add the potatoes, peas (or beans), herbs and stock. Bring to the boil, reduce the heat and simmer for 20-25 minutes until the potatoes are soft.

Meanwhile, about five minutes before the soup is ready, put the other 2 tbsp oil in a frying pan with two cloves of finely chopped garlic (optional) and add the extra chopped leaves. Stir fry for 4-5 minutes.

When the soup is cooked, purée using an immersion blender and season to taste.

Serve with sautéed greens and a sprinkle of fresh herbs on top.

TIP   In the summer, replace 1 cup of beans with a cup of diced cucumber or courgette.

Kale and czar bean soup

This delicious soup is eaten without blending so be sure to cut the vegetables into bite-sized pieces.

480g (17oz/3 cups) cooked beans

135g (4¾oz/1 cup) onions, chopped

150g (5oz/1 cup) carrots, chopped

180g (5¼oz/4 cups) kale, shredded

120g (4oz/1 cup) celery, thinly sliced

2-4 cloves garlic, according to taste

1.2 litres (42fl.oz/8 cups) vegetable stock

1 tbsp rosemary leaves, finely chopped (keep the stalks)

½ tbsp thyme leaves, finely chopped (keep the stalks)

2 tbsp parsley, finely chopped, including the stalks

2 tbsp olive oil

Salt and pepper to taste

Make a herb bundle made from two bay leaves, the herb stalks and an additional sprig of rosemary and thyme tied with food grade string.

Put the olive oil in the soup pan and add the onions, celery and garlic. Sauté on a low heat until the onions have softened, then add the carrots, kale, beans, herbs and herb bundle. Pour over the stock, bring to the boil and simmer for 30 minutes.

Remove the herb bundle and compost. Taste and season the soup before serving.

SUMMER VARIATION

Replace 4 cups of the stock with chopped tomatoes. Replace the chopped rosemary and thyme leaves with basil and oregano.

Use up your glut courgette soup

You can use courgettes that have decided to turn into marrows in this soup – just peel and deseed before use. I like to make this with summer squash too. It's a great way of making something light and delicious from the seemingly never ending glut of courgettes!

The soup keeps for two or three days in the fridge and freezes well.

1.2kg (42oz/8 cups) courgette, diced

270g (9½oz/2 cups) onions, chopped

1 litre (35fl.oz/4¼ cups) stock

2 cloves garlic (more if you like it)

120g (4oz/1 cup) celery

2 tbsp olive oil

2 tbsp chopped basil, parsley or mint (or a mixture of all three) with some extra to garnish

OPTIONAL TOPPING

1 courgette, cut into circles

1 clove garlic, finely chopped

2 tbsp oil

Put the oil in the soup pan, add the onion, celery and garlic and sauté until the onion is soft. Add the courgette, stir and then add the stock and herbs and bring to the boil. Reduce the heat and simmer for 20 minutes.

Meanwhile, make the topping (if desired). Put the oil in the pan, add the courgette, seeds and garlic and sauté until the courgette is cooked.

When the soup is ready, blend with an immersion blender. Taste and season.

Serve topped with the sautéed courgette mix, or sprinkle with fresh herbs.

SUMMER VARIATION

Replace 2 cups of stock with 2 cups of chopped tomatoes.

CREAMY VARIATION

Replace 2 cups of stock with coconut milk. Add 1 finely chopped chilli to the ingredients for a light spicy kick.

Taste of North Africa roasted aubergine and tomato soup

For a few short weeks each year, I have a wonderful glut of aubergines. This is a magical time for me because I adore aubergines and they take so long to grow in the UK. I grow at least 15 different varieties at home, sowing the seeds around Valentines Day indoors in heated propagators. Each plant needs keeping frost free until they can be planted in the polytunnel in mid-May or the more hardy varieties outside in early June. It is a real labour of love!

This soup is also delicious made with aubergines bought in season from shops and markets.

I always fill the oven with several trays of roasted vegetables, to make this soup and as a base for salads and other meals.

Preheat the oven to 180ºC fan (200ºC/400ºF/gas mark 6).

Spread the aubergines, onions, tomatoes and garlic on the oven trays, drizzle with olive oil (the aubergines will need more than the onions and tomatoes) and put in the oven for 25 minutes until the aubergines are cooked through.

Put the cooked vegetables in a soup pan and add the stock, spices and herbs. Bring to the boil, reduce the heat and simmer for 20 minutes. After 15 minutes, stir through the tahini and lemon juice.

Season to taste. I love this soup puréed or served as it is, so the choice is yours!

Sprinkle with fresh herbs. This is gorgeous with garlic bread.

400g (14¾oz/4 cups) aubergines, diced, any kind

120g (4oz/2 cups) onions, diced

1 whole head garlic

350g (12¼oz) cherry tomatoes, cut in half (or diced larger tomatoes)

500ml (17½fl.oz/2¾ cups) stock (plus more water if needed)

3 tbsp tahini

1 lemon, juice (optional)

½ tsp cayenne

½ tsp ground cumin

1 tbsp Za'atar style spice mix (page 22)

Fresh basil or parsley

Olive oil

Warming winter roasted celeriac and parsnip soup

Roasting the vegetables so that they are almost caramelised really brings out their deep, sweet flavours. If you roast more than you need, the veggies make a great base for many other meals and a delicious pâté (see page 105).

500g (17½oz/3½ cups) parsnip, peeled and diced

500g (17½oz/3½ cups) celeriac, peeled and diced

135g (4¾oz/1 cup) onions, cut into eighths

300g (10½oz/3 cups) leeks, cut into 2cm pieces

1½ litres (53fl.oz/6½ cups) stock or water

Olive oil

2 cloves garlic (more if you like it), finely chopped

1 or 2 chillies (optional)

A bundle of winter herbs

2 tbsp fresh parsley, chopped, plus more to garnish

Salt and pepper to taste

Preheat the oven to 180°C fan (200°C/400°F/gas mark 6).

Spread the parsnip, celeriac, onions and leeks on a baking tray, drizzle with olive oil and roast for 30 minutes until soft.

Remove from the oven and transfer the contents of the tray to your soup pan. Be sure to scrape everything including the oil in. Add the garlic, chillies (if using), herb bundle, parsley and stock. Bring to the boil, reduce heat and simmer for 30 minutes. Remove the herb bundle and purée using an immersion blender. Taste and season.

Serve sprinkled with fresh parsley.

Fresh Florence fennel and carrot soup

260g (9oz/2 cups) carrots, sliced

300g (10½oz) approx. large fennel bulb (or 2 small), chopped

70g (2½oz/½ cup) onions or leeks, sliced

2 stalks celery, sliced

1 tsp fennel seed (optional), lightly toasted

1 litre (35fl.oz/4¼ cups) vegetable stock

1 tbsp oil

Fennel fronds to garnish (optional)

Salt and pepper to taste

OPTIONAL

Replace 120ml (4fl.oz/½ cup) of stock with juice and zest of 1 orange

Pour the oil into the soup pan and sauté the onions and celery until softened.

Add the carrots and fennel, stir and pour over the vegetable stock. Bring to the boil, reduce heat and simmer for 20 minutes until the fennel and carrots are soft.

Taste and season as desired.

I like this soup served with the vegetables floating in the broth. For a creamy soup, purée using an immersion blender.

Serve garnished with a sprinkle of toasted fennel seeds and fennel fronds.

3
SALADS

Salade Repas is the idea of salads as a main meal; a selection of fresh, seasonal dishes eaten together to create jewel coloured meals. Many of the salads here make a complete meal in themselves, but I like to make several different dishes at a time along with salsas and pickles. Lasting for several days in the fridge, there's always a delicious, colourful, healthy meal ready.

At our Homeacres gardening courses, I make between 10 and 14 different homegrown seasonal salads in a morning for lunch; at home it is more usually three or four at a time. We serve them with fresh bread and seasonal salad leaves.

These salads lend themselves beautifully to a quick bowlful at home, or layered in jars to take for packed lunches and suppers. I like to eat salads for breakfast too.

Raw vegetable carpaccio with beetroot dip

A stunning rainbow feast, serve with hummus.

FOR THE RAW BEETROOT DIP

200g (7oz/1¼ cup) raw beetroot

4 tbsp tahini

1 lemon, juice and zest

1 tsp ground cumin

1 tsp ground coriander

1 tbsp olive oil

2 tsp coriander or parsley, chopped (plus more to decorate)

Salt and pepper to taste

Finely grate the beetroot (I use the finest grate on my food processor) and place into a blender or food processor.

Add the other ingredients and blend. Add a little water if necessary.

TIP   If you prefer a sweeter dip, replace 50g of the beetroot with finely grated apple.

FOR THE CARPACCIO

Your choice of raw seasonal vegetables and fruit:

Chioggia beetroot (for the amazing pink and white stripes)

Yellow beetroot

Carrot – any colour you like

Florence fennel

Cucumber

Courgette

Tomatoes

Radish

Kohl rabi

Pear

Apple

Summer squash

Cauliflower

Broccoli

Red onion

Spring onions

Fresh herbs – according to the season

DRESSING

160ml (5½fl.oz/⅔ cup) olive oil

60ml (2fl.oz/¼ cup) lemon juice

Pinch of sea salt and black pepper

Finely slice your vegetables and arrange on the serving platter. Sprinkle with herbs of your choice. I like to vary them according to the vegetable, so dill or mint on the cucumber and basil or French tarragon on the tomatoes.

Whisk the dressing ingredients together and drizzle over the vegetables.

Summer berry salsa

Apples, pears, plums and other fruit also work well with this colourful salsa.

180g (6¼oz/2 cups) seasonal berries (raspberries, gooseberries, strawberries, blackberries, redcurrants, blackcurrants, whitecurrants, blueberries)

1 red onion, finely chopped (or spring onions, including the green)

1 or 2 chilli peppers, deseeded and finely chopped

1 lime, juice and zest

3 tbsp coriander, chopped

Put all of the ingredients in a bowl and mix carefully together.

Tomatillo (or gooseberry) salsa verde

Every year I look forward to the first ripe tomatillos so I can make salsa verde. Quick to make, it lasts for a week in the fridge and is a delicious accompaniment to many dishes.

If you do not have any tomatillos, replace them with green tomatoes, or gooseberries with finely chopped green peppers. It'll taste good but different. I can't grow it here in Somerset, but roasted pineapple is good in this recipe too!

500g (17½oz) tomatillos (approx. 8-9)

4 spring onions, chopped, including the greens (or white or red onions)

1 tbsp coriander leaves

2 tbsp parsley

1 tbsp basil

2-4 cloves garlic, crushed

1 lime, juice and zest

1-2 chillies, deseeded and chopped (optional)

2 tbsp olive oil

1 tbsp country capers (or bought ones)

Salt and pepper to taste

Preheat the oven to 180°C fan (200°C/400°F/gas mark 6).

Remove the husk from the tomatillos and arrange on an oven dish, drizzle with olive oil and season. Roast for 15-20 minutes until soft. Remove from the oven and allow to cool for 10 minutes.

Finely chop everything and mix together (I do this in a large pestle and mortar, but a bowl and wooden spoon is fine), or add all of the ingredients to a food processor and blend until there are just small chunks.

Taste before seasoning.

Gooseberry and green pepper variation – replace the tomatillos with:

250g (9oz) gooseberries

250g (9oz) green peppers

Deseed and quarter the green peppers. Drizzle with some oil and put in the oven for five minutes. Add the gooseberries to the pan with a little more oil. Roast for a further 15 minutes until soft.

Prepare the salsa verde as above.

Raw purple sprouting broccoli salad

Purple sprouting broccoli quickly becomes very abundant at my allotment, so I enjoy creating as many different dishes as possible with this seasonal treat. I am happy to eat the chopped stems too, but if you find those too chewy, use more florets and reserve the stems for stocks; or steam and serve like asparagus.

500g (17½oz /6 cups) purple sprouting broccoli shoots (or just the florets if you prefer)

135g (4¾oz /1 cup) red onion, finely sliced and chopped (or use spring onions)

130g (4½oz /1 cup) pumpkin seeds or sunflower seeds, cashews, almonds)

DRESSING

65g (2¼oz/½ cup) cashews or almonds

60g (2oz/½ cup) sunflower seeds

65g (2¼oz/½ cup) pumpkin seeds

1-2 cloves garlic, minced

½ lemon, juice

1 tbsp cider vinegar

3 tbsp olive oil

Salt and pepper to taste

Water for soaking nuts/seeds (plus more if needed)

Put the nuts and seeds into a bowl, pour over enough water to cover by 2cm and leave for 30 minutes or so to soak.

Drain, reserving the soaking liquid.

Put the soaked nuts and seeds into a blender or food processor. Add the other dressing ingredients along with ⅔ cup of the soaking liquid and blend, adding more soaking liquid or water as required, until the dressing resembles pouring cream.

Place the broccoli, onions and seeds (or nuts) in a bowl, pour over the dressing and mix carefully.

In season, replace the purple sprouting broccoli with raw calabrese or cauliflower florets.

Roast purple sprouting broccoli salad

Try this salad with roasted calabrese or cauliflower florets, or bite sized chunks of cabbage. It is delicious warm and cool and keeps for three days in the fridge. The salad makes a tasty topping for pasta, couscous or rice.

800g (28oz) purple sprouting broccoli, cut into florets and the stems into 3cm lengths

2 red onions, sliced

2 tbsp olive oil

100g (3½oz) pumpkin or sunflower seeds

DRESSING

2 cloves garlic, finely minced (more if you like garlic)

1 cup tahini

1 lemon, juice and zest

Salt and pepper to taste

1 cup water (plus more as needed)

Preheat the oven to 180°C fan (200°C/400°F/gas mark 6).

Prepare the vegetables and spread on an oven tray. Drizzle with olive oil, mixing to make sure everything is coated and put in the oven. Roast for 30 minutes.

Meanwhile, put the dressing ingredients in a bowl or blender and mix thoroughly, adding a little more water if necessary, until the creamy dressing resembles pouring cream.

Spread the seeds on a baking tray. Pop in the oven three minutes before the vegetables are cooked and dry roast, shaking the tray occasionally to make sure they don't burn.

When everything has cooked, put the vegetables and seeds into a bowl. Add the dressing, mixing carefully, and either serve warm or allow to cool before eating.

Steamed purple sprouting broccoli and roast vegetable salad

This recipe combines steamed broccoli and leftover roasted vegetables. I always roast more veg than I need for a meal – having a bowl of leftovers in the fridge means this colourful and flavoursome salad is quick to assemble.

500g (17½oz) purple sprouting broccoli, cut into bite sized pieces

500g (17½oz) roasted vegetables, whatever you have, depending on the season – onions, squash, parsnips, potato, sweet potato, turnip, leeks, celeriac, swede, courgette, sweet pepper …

TAHINI DRESSING

136ml (4¾fl.oz/1 cup) tahini

1 lemon, juice

136ml (4¾fl.oz/1 cup) of water

Salt and pepper to taste

Make the dressing by whisking the ingredients together or blending in a food processor. It should resemble thick cream. Add a little more water if necessary, taste and season.

Steam the broccoli for 4-5 minutes until tender, drain (reserving the liquid for soups, etc.) and cool.

Mix the broccoli with the roasted vegetables, place in a bowl and pour over the dressing.

TIP Add a cup of czar beans or soaked nuts before mixing the vegetables, to make this salad into a substantial meal.

Roast beetroot salad with walnuts

500g (17½oz/4 cups) beetroot, any colour, diced

270g (8½oz/2 cups) onions, cut into eighths

125g (4½oz/1 cup) carrots, diced

125g (4½oz/1 cup) parsnips, diced

Olive oil

100g (3½oz/1 cup) walnuts, broken

2 oranges, peeled and diced or 2 apples, cored and diced (optional)

ORANGE VINAIGRETTE

2 oranges, juice and zest

6 tbsp olive oil

2 tsp Dijon mustard

2 tbsp apple balsamic vinegar
(or cider or red wine vinegar)

1 tbsp fresh thyme, chopped

1 tbsp fresh French tarragon, chopped
(plus a little extra for a topping)

Salt and pepper to taste

VARIATIONS

Replace any or all of the root vegetables with other seasonal veg: kohl rabi, radish, mooli, celeriac, turnip.

Replace the onions with leeks, sliced into 2cm rings.

Replace the walnuts with cashews, pecans, hazelnuts, almonds, sunflower seeds or pumpkin seeds.

Preheat the oven to 180°C fan (200°C/400°F/gas mark 6).

Spread the vegetables on an ovenproof dish and drizzle with olive oil. Wiggle the vegetables with your fingers to coat with the oil, or use a spatula. Place in the oven for 20-25 minutes until cooked through, checking occasionally to make sure they are cooking evenly.

Meanwhile, make the salad dressing by mixing all of the ingredients together in a jug.

Spread the walnuts on a baking tray.

Remove the vegetables from the oven when they are ready and leave to cool.

Put the tray of walnuts into the oven for 3-4 minutes. Check every minute, moving the walnuts about by shaking the tray carefully to make sure they don't burn. Walnuts quickly turn from perfectly toasted to burnt to a frazzle, so do keep an eye on them. They will have browned a little and smell richly of walnut. When cooked, remove from the oven and carefully tip onto a plate to cool.

If you prefer, you can add the nuts raw.

When everything has cooled, place the vegetables, nuts and fruit (if using) in a mixing bowl. Pour over some of the dressing, stir, repeating until everything has been coated with the vinaigrette. Store any leftover vinaigrette in a lidded jar in the fridge for a week, it's delicious on salad.

Spoon into the serving bowl and sprinkle with finely chopped French tarragon.

Deep red beetroot salad with toasted pumpkin seeds

This simple salad is one of Charles' favourites, I think he could eat it every day!

300g (10oz/2 cups) raw red beetroot, grated

150g (5oz/1 cup) raw apple, grated (cored but leave skin on)

130g (4½oz/1 cup) pumpkin seeds

DRESSING

2 tbsp cider vinegar

4 tbsp olive oil

2 tsp wholegrain mustard

2 tbsp fresh chervil, finely chopped (plus more for decoration)

Whisk the dressing together.

Mix the grated apple, beetroot and chervil together.

Put the pumpkin seeds, spread on a baking tray, in the oven at 180°C. Cook for three minutes, checking regularly and skaking the tray so that they don't burn. Sometimes they'll make a 'popping' sound: this is quite normal.

Remove from the oven and cool. Check that there are no escapee pumpkin seeds at the bottom of your oven. Sometimes I find that they can 'pop' with such enthusiasm some fly over the edge of the oven tray!

Alternatively, use raw pumpkin seeds.

Add the pumpkin seeds to the salad, pour over the dressing and mix. Place in the serving dish and sprinkle more finely chopped chervil over the top.

Raw grated golden beetroot 'sunshine' salad

This is such a bright yellow-orange colour that it always reminds us of sunshine. It's especially welcome in the depths of winter, using stored root vegetables.

150g (5oz/1 cup) golden beetroot, grated

150g (5oz/1 cup) carrot, grated

150g (5oz/1 cup) kohl rabi, grated

2 tbsp fresh parsley, chervil, French tarragon or mint to decorate, finely chopped (optional)

DRESSING

Lemon, mint and parsley (page 24)
or
Orange vinaigrette (page 62)

Grate the vegetables and mix together in a roomy bowl. Gradually pour on the dressing until thoroughly mixed.

Transfer into the serving bowl and sprinkle the finely chopped herbs on top, if desired.

TIP   To make this salad more of a complete meal, add a cup of nuts or seeds of your choice.

ALTERNATIVE   Vegetables and fruit: celeriac, parsley, turnip, swede, apple, pear.

raw grated golden beetroot 'sunshine' salad

Candy pink salad

I like to use a middle-sized grater to make this, so that the candy stripes are clearly visible. This is light and very pretty. Serve with Turnip and Raspberry salad (page 69) for more pink and white summery-ness.

2 Chioggia beetroot

DRESSING 3 tbsp olive oil

1 tbsp red wine vinegar (white wine or cider vinegar is good too)

Simply peel and grate the beetroot, then mix with the dressing.

Two simple, delicious ways to use cooked czar beans and fresh herbs

I mostly grow czar beans, but you can use any white bean in these recipes.

Czar beans and herbs

I serve this as part of our course lunches so that people can taste czar beans in a more simple form and hopefully feel inspired to grow them at home. It always vanishes!

This salad is useful to have in the fridge. It's a delicious addition to the vegetable salads for lunch jars and is great stirred through pasta for a quick meal.

I vary the herbs according to what I have growing – mint, dill, parsley, lemon verbena, lemon balm and French tarragon are all delicious.

240g (8½oz/1½ cups) cooked beans

1 tbsp herbs, finely chopped

2 tbsp lemon vinaigrette
(see page 24)

Simply mix together.

Czar bean and herb pâté

The ingredients are exactly the same as the czar bean and herb salad.

Place in a food processor and blend until creamy. Add a little water if necessary to make a smooth pâté.

Serve: with crusty bread, as a sandwich filling with salad leaves, with crudités, vegetable carpaccio, drizzled on top of roasted vegetables, stirred into sauces, fill a baked potato …

Herby potato salad

Charles and I differ when it comes to potatoes – I love to eat the skin, he prefers to remove it. The light, fresh dressing makes this a year round favourite – make it skin on or off, whichever you prefer.

500g (17½oz) potatoes
3 tbsp oil
1 tbsp cider vinegar
2 tsp dijon mustard
2-3 tbsp herbs, freshly chopped
Salt and pepper to taste

Boil the potatoes until cooked, drain (reserving the cooking water for soups etc.) and cool.

Meanwhile, make the dressing.

When the potatoes are cooled, mix with the salad dressing and serve.

For hot potato salad, stir through the salad dressing after draining and serve.

Zesty raw parsnip salad

This light, fresh tasting salad is just what is needed during dark winter months. People are often surprised when I serve it and have usually not tried raw parsnip before, but it quickly becomes a favourite.

It is delicious made with just parsnip (in which case, simply double the quantity of grated parsnip) but I like to add celeriac for an extra flavour dimension.

This recipe is best made a couple of hours before you wish to eat it.

150g (5oz/1 cup) parsnip, grated

150g (5oz/1 cup) celeriac, grated

DRESSING

½ lemon, juice and zest

½ lime, juice and zest

8 tbsp olive oil

Freshly chopped parsley (or mint, lemon verbena, French tarragon, lemon balm) with extra to decorate

I grate the vegetables using the finest blade on my food processor.

Whisk the dressing together and mix with the grated vegetables in a roomy bowl, gently pounding the root veg and dressing, and mixing together as you do, for a few minutes. This really helps to get the zingy dressing thoroughly into the vegetables and also softens them a little.

Place in the serving bowl, sprinkle with herbs and put in a cool place until serving.

Turnip and raspberry salad

This pretty salad resembles a dessert! The sweet, crisp turnip tastes fantastic with raspberries.

300g (10oz/2 cups) white turnips, grated

150g (5oz/1 cup) raspberries

DRESSING

2 tbsp raspberry vinegar*

6 tbsp olive oil

*   Or use rose petal vinegar, cider or white wine vinegar instead.

Whisk the raspberry vinegar and olive oil together.

Carefully mix the grated turnip and raspberries together, with the dressing.

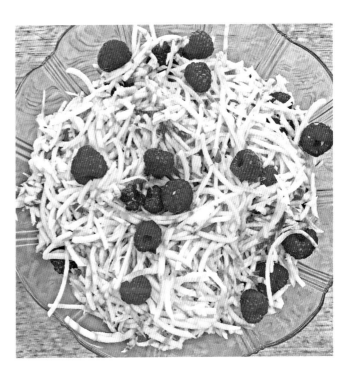

Fresh chard summer salad with carlin peas

Include the thinner vibrantly coloured chard stalks in this salad, but any large stalks may be too chewy. Reserve these to add to soups, curries and other cooked meals. Or, thinly slice, steam until soft and add to this salad.

Carlin peas are easy to grow and also available dried and in tins (see Resources on page 120). Alternatively, replace with other dried peas, or cooked beans, cooked or sprouted chickpeas, or nuts and seeds.

1 bunch chard, shredded
(roughly 450g/16oz)

12 cherry tomatoes, cut in half

½ cucumber, halved and sliced

6 radishes, sliced

½ cup red onion, thinly sliced or spring onions

1 sweet pepper, thinly sliced

240g (8½ oz/1½ cups) cooked carlin peas

2 tbsp parsley, finely chopped

2 tbsp basil, finely chopped

DRESSING

3 tbsp olive oil

1 tbsp lemon juice

1 clove garlic, finely chopped

Salt and pepper to taste

Crunchy chard, apple and walnut salad

I use young small leaves of chard in this salad, but you can use larger leaves, removing any tougher stalks. Alternatively, replace with beetroot leaves, spinach or mixed salad leaves.

For a sweeter salad, add a handful or two of sultanas.

200g (7oz) raw baby chard including the stems, shredded

2 apples, cored and diced

125g (4½oz/1 cup) walnuts, raw or toasted

2 stems celery, sliced

Fresh parsley to decorate (optional)

DRESSING

1 clove garlic, minced

6 tbsp olive oil

2 tbsp cider vinegar

1 tsp dijon mustard

Salt and pepper to taste

Whisk the dressing ingredients together until emulsified.

Put the salad ingredients into a bowl and pour over the dressing. Mix carefully, put in the dish and serve sprinkled with parsley.

crunchy chard, apple and walnut salad

spiced chard salad

Spiced chard salad

This is tasty warm and cold. I love it warm over rice noodles or couscous as a quick lunch or supper. Add a cup of peanuts, chickpeas, beans or peas for a more filling salad.

1 bunch chard, shredded
(roughly 450g/16oz)

150g (5oz/1 cup) carrot, grated
(or other root vegetable – golden
beetroot, parsnip, turnip, celeriac)

2-4 cloves garlic

2 tbsp sunflower oil

2 tbsp lemon, orange or lime juice
(as you fancy!)

1-2 tsp Za'atar style spices

Salt and pepper to taste

Coriander, basil or parsley to serve,
chopped

Put the oil in a pan and add the chard, garlic, spices and grated carrot. Stir until the vegetables are cooked through and soft, about 10 minutes.

Add the citrus juice and stir. Season to taste, sprinkle over the herbs and stir.

Roast onion salad with wild garlic pesto

This salad is delicious made with shallots, spring onions and leeks. It's a good way of using up any over-wintered onions, which seem to start bolting around the same time that the wild garlic is in season.

8 medium-sized red onions (white are
fine too)

2 tbsp olive oil

Balsamic vinegar (or a fruit vinegar of your
choice, blackcurrant is good) to drizzle

A sprinkle of salt and pepper (optional)

WILD GARLIC PESTO

100g (3½oz/1 cup) walnuts

150g (5oz) wild garlic

2 cloves garlic, minced

6 tbsp walnut oil (olive or sunflower)

2 tbsp lemon juice

A little water, as needed

When wild garlic is not in season, replace with rocket for a spicy pesto or spinach for a milder pesto.

Preheat the oven to 180°C fan (200°C/400°F/gas mark 6).

Peel the onions and cut in half. Arrange on an ovenproof dish and brush the olive oil all over to coat. Roast in the centre of the oven for 20 minutes until the onions are soft and cooked. Remove from the oven and sprinkle with a little balsamic vinegar (and salt and pepper if you wish).

Whilst the onions are cooking, make the pesto. Place the walnuts, wild garlic, minced garlic, oil and lemon juice in a food processor. Blend, adding a little water if necessary, to make a thick sauce.

Eat the onion salad hot or cold, drizzling the pesto over the onions before serving.

If you prefer, cut the onions into quarters before roasting and reduce the cooking time to around 15 minutes.

Fennel and swede coleslaw

I use a food processor with a medium-sized blade to make this winter salad. If swede is not in season, replace it with golden beetroot, kohl rabi or carrot. In the summer, try using sweet white turnips or grated courgettes.

300g (10oz/2 cups) swede, grated

300g (10oz/2 cups) fennel, shredded

1 apple, grated

2 tbsp fennel seeds, toasted or raw (optional)

Fennel fronds to decorate

DRESSING

6 tbsp olive oil

2 tbsp cider or white wine vinegar

1 tsp Dijon mustard

Salt and pepper to taste

Whisk the salad dressing together.

Place the vegetables in a bowl, pour over the dressing and mix so that all of the vegetables are coated.

Put into the serving dish and decorate with fennel fronds and seeds.

Garlic and ginger bean salad

When the beans are not in season, replace the French beans with cooked purple sprouting broccoli or steamed chopped chard, including the stems. Use onions or leeks in place of the spring onions and grated carrot or apple to replace the sweet pepper.
This recipe works well with defrosted or canned French beans too.

450g (16oz) fresh French beans, cut into 4-5cm pieces

2 spring onions, finely sliced

1 sweet pepper, finely sliced

DRESSING

3 tbsp sunflower oil

2 cloves garlic, finely chopped

1 tsp fresh ginger, finely chopped

1 chilli, deseeded and finely chopped (optional)

2 tbsp tamari (or other soy sauce)

2 tbsp lime juice (or lemon juice, or cider vinegar)

2 tbsp fresh chopped basil, parsley or coriander

Bring a large pan of water to the boil, add the beans and cook for 3-4 minutes until cooked through but still crisp.

Drain and rinse with icy cold water to cool quickly and transfer to a bowl.

Whisk the dressing to combine and pour over the beans. Add the finely chopped spring onions and sweet pepper and stir.

Serve sprinkled with the chopped herbs.

Dilly bean salad

I like to use a combination of green and yellow French beans in this salad. Runner beans are delicious too.

450g (16oz) fresh French beans

3 tbsp olive oil

1 tbsp lemon juice or cider vinegar

1 tsp wholegrain mustard

2 tbsp fresh dill, finely chopped

Salt and pepper to taste

Cut the beans into 4-5cm pieces. I usually just snap them in half.

Bring a large pan of water to the boil, add the beans and cook for 3-4 minutes until cooked through but still crisp.

Drain and rinse with icy cold water to cool quickly and transfer to a bowl.

Whisk the dressing to combine and pour over the beans. Stir to coat all of the beans with the dill dressing and serve.

VARIATION

Replace the dill with 2 tbsp chopped French tarragon.

Roast rhubarb salad with fruity balsamic dressing

A rhubarb salad may sound a little bizarre but honestly, this is really good. The tartness of the rhubarb is offset with the sweet dressing and the sweet flavours of the roasted vegetables.

This salad combines newly harvested beetroot with the summer flavours of your homemade fruit vinegars. If you don't have any home-made vinegars, replace with balsamic or a shop bought fruit vinegar.

500g (17½oz) beetroot, various colours, diced

250g (9oz) carrots, diced

250g (9oz) red or white onions, cut into eighths

500g (17½oz) rhubarb, cut into 5cm pieces

Olive oil

FRUITY BALSAMIC SALAD DRESSING

8 tbsp olive oil

4 tbsp homemade fruit balsamic vinegar (see page 26)

2 tbsp organic juice (or lemon, or lime)

2 tbsp fresh chervil, French tarragon or parsley to serve, finely chopped

Preheat the oven to 180°C fan (200°C/400°F/gas mark 6).

Place the diced beetroot, carrots and onions on a baking tray and coat with a little oil. Roast for 20-25 minutes until the vegetables are cooked through.

Meanwhile, spread the rhubarb on another tray and brush with oil. After 10 minutes add the rhubarb and bake for 10-12 minutes, until cooked and soft but not mushy.

Allow the vegetables to cool.

Mix the dressing together. Place the cooled vegetables in a bowl and carefully mix with the dressing.

Sprinkle with the fresh herbs to serve.

TIP   If you want a sweeter dressing to accompany the rhubarb salad, add 1-2 tbsp of maple syrup (to taste).

Raw fennel and apple salsa with lime vinaigrette

A bright fresh autumn salad, when summer sown Florence fennel and apples are both in season.

1 bulb Florence fennel

2 crisp apples, grated

4 medium-sized tomatoes, diced

3 spring onions, finely sliced

DRESSING

3 tbsp sunflower or olive oil

2 limes, juice and zest

1 clove garlic, minced

1 chilli, deseeded and finely chopped (optional)

2 tbsp chopped fresh coriander

Salt and pepper to taste

Fennel fronds to decorate, finely chopped (if you wish)

Whisk the dressing together or shake in a lidded jam jar.

Finely shred the fennel using a sharp kitchen knife, mandolin or food processor. Place in a bowl with the apples, tomatoes and spring onions.

Pour over the dressing and stir to combine.

ALTERNATIVE

Replace the lime with lemon or an infused cider or wine vinegar.

Raw massaged kale salad

This is a delicious and easy way of eating raw kale. It's lovely as a topping on other salads and always surprises people who have never tried kale raw before!

A big bunch of kale, any kind – more than you think you'll need!

A drizzle of olive oil

Salt and pepper

Clean hands!

Some good music to listen to for 10 minutes

Remove the kale from the stalks and rip into 5cm pieces with your fingers. Place in a bowl and sprinkle with some salt.

Put on the music.

Massage the kale for about 10 minutes, using the pressure one would for a gentle neck massage. The kale will soften, darken and reduce. That big bowl of leaves will diminish into more of a soup bowl quantity.

Drizzle on a little olive oil and a sprinkle of pepper and rub through with your fingers. It's now ready to serve.

Roasted crispy kale

A big bunch of kale, any kind

Olive oil

Preheat the oven to 200°C fan (220°C/428°F/gas mark 7).

Remove the leaves from the stalks and rip into 5cm pieces. Place on an oven tray, drizzle over a little oil and lightly coat the kale with your fingers.

Put in the oven for 10-12 minutes, checking occasionally to make sure it is evenly cooked. You may need to move the kale around the dish with a wooden spatula.

When cooked and crispy, remove from the oven and allow to cool.

I like the kale just like this. If you prefer, sprinkle on a little smoked paprika or tamarin before serving.

TIP Reserve the kale stalks to add to your homemade stocks.

Som tum vegetable salads

Whenever I visit Thailand, where my Dad lives, I look forward to eating this very hot and spicy salad. Traditionally made with green papaya, which can be bought from speciality international shops in the UK, at home I have adapted the dish to include seasonal vegetables and less spiciness.

I have the traditional Thai pestle and mortar for pounding and mixing the spices and the salad itself. The name Som Tum comes from the pounding of the salad in a pestle and mortar. A large bowl and a wooden spoon will be fine too.

A julienne peeler is ideal for preparing this salad, I have some simple Thai graters, or use a mandolin or food processor.

Serve with quick pickled chillies so that everyone can choose their own degree of chilli kick!

Som Tum is traditionally made with an added sweetener, such as palm sugar. I prefer these sugar free versions, however if you would like more sweetness in your dish, add 2 tbsp palm sugar or 1 tbsp regular sugar to the dressing.

Winter som tum

115g (4oz/1 cup) unsalted roasted peanuts (or raw if you prefer)

150g (5oz/1 cup) parsnip, grated

150g (5oz/1 cup) swede, grated

150g (5oz/1 cup) cabbage, grated

150g (5oz/1 cup) kohl rabi, grated

2-4 garlic cloves, according to taste, chopped

1-2 Thai chillies

1 tbsp coriander stems and roots, chopped (if you have them)

3 tbsp fresh coriander leaves or parsley

Wedges of lime and fresh shredded salad leaves to serve (optional)

DRESSING

¼ cup lime or lemon juice

1 tbsp tamari or soy sauce

Salt and pepper to taste

Deseed (if you want to reduce the heat) and chop the chillies. Put in a pestle and mortar with the garlic cloves and coriander roots/stems. Add a little salt and carefully pound to make a paste. Protect your eyes and be careful not to touch anywhere sensitive until you have washed your hands. Add half of the peanuts and crush.

Whisk the dressing together.

Place the grated vegetables in the pestle and mortar (if large enough) or put in a sturdy bowl with the chilli paste. Pour over the dressing, mix thoroughly using a spatula or wooden spoon and then gently pound the salad with the mortar or a large wooden spoon or rolling pin, using the spatula to turn the salad as you pound. The idea is to bruise the salad ingredients, rather than pounding into a pulp. This takes 3-4 minutes.

Place the shredded leaves on the serving dish and add the Som Tum. Sprinkle with the coriander leaves and peanuts.

Serve with wedges of lime and quick pickled chillies for those who prefer this a little spicier.

VARIATIONS

Replace the root vegetables with:
golden Chioggia or white beetroot, kohl rabi, carrots, celeriac.

Summer som tum

115g (4oz/1 cup) unsalted roasted peanuts (or raw if you prefer)

160g (5½oz/1 cup) cucumber, grated

150g (5oz/1 cup) carrot, grated

150g (5oz/1 cup) courgette, grated

115g (4oz/1 cup) sweet pepper, any colour, seed removed and sliced

75g (2½oz/½ cup) cherry tomatoes, halved

75g (2½oz/½ cup) French beans, cut into 4cm pieces

2-4 garlic cloves, according to taste, chopped

1-2 Thai chillies, according to taste

1 tbsp coriander stems and roots, chopped (if you have them)

3 tbsp fresh coriander leaves or basil – Thai basil if you have it

Wedges of lime and fresh shredded salad leaves to serve (optional)

DRESSING

3 tbsp lime or lemon juice

1 tbsp tamari or soy sauce

Salt and pepper to taste

Prepare the salad following the method for Winter Som Tum, but leave the tomatoes out until just before serving so that they don't get squashed.

VARIATIONS
Replace some or all of the vegetables with: radishes, courgette, summer cabbage, summer squash, apple, pear.

winter som tum

Quick pickled chillies

100g (3½oz/1 cup) chillies, sliced with seeds

236ml (8fl.oz/1 cup) cider or white wine vinegar

236ml (8fl.oz/1 cup) water

2 cloves garlic, finely chopped

2 tbsp unbleached sugar

1 tbsp salt

Hot sterilised jars with lids

Place the vinegar, water, sugar, garlic and salt in a pan. Bring to the boil and carefully add the chillies. Remove the pan from the heat, stir and leave for 10 minutes.

Using a slotted spoon, fill the jars with the chillies and carefully pour over the hot liquid. Seal.

This can be eaten right away or stored in the fridge for 6-8 weeks.

North African parsnip salad

This salad reminds me of some of the meals we had in Morocco, none of which included parsnip but the spices and dried fruits take me back to a beautiful walled city beside the ocean.

450g (15oz/3 cups) parsnip, grated

150g (5oz/1 cup) carrots, grated

1 tsp coriander seeds

1 tsp cumin seeds

1 tsp fennel seeds

½ tsp ground cinnamon

175g (6oz/1 cup) dried dates, figs or apricots, chopped

2 tbsp coriander, chopped

2 tbsp mint, chopped

110g (4oz/½ cup) almonds, toasted or raw

1 lemon, juice

6 tbsp olive oil

Salt and pepper to taste

A little extra chopped fresh herbs to decorate

Place the coriander, cumin and fennel seeds in a frying pan and toast for about two minutes, stirring continually. Transfer to a pestle and mortar or small blender. Add the cinnamon and grind the spices to a powder.

Whisk together the lemon juice, olive oil, spices and a little salt and pepper.

Put the grated vegetables into a bowl. Add the dried fruit, almonds, mint and coriander. Pour over the dressing and stir to combine.

Serve sprinkled with fresh herbs and a pot of mint tea.

VARIATIONS

Replace the parsnip and/or carrots with grated celeriac, turnip, courgette, apple, kohl rabi, cabbage, cucumber, radish.

Use raisins or sultanas in place of the dates.

Replace the almonds with any nut of your choice, sunflower or pumpkin seeds.

Roast radish and kale salad

1 bunch of radish – about 12

115g (4oz/2 cups) kale, shredded

2 cloves garlic, sliced

Olive oil

Salt and pepper to taste

Preheat the oven to 180°C fan (200°C/400°F/gas mark 6).

Cut the leaves off the radish, leaving 4-5cm of stalk. Cut the radishes in half.

Spread the kale over an ovenproof dish and drizzle over some oil. Coat the kale using your fingers or a brush. Place the radish on top of the kale, drizzle with oil and season with salt and pepper.

Put in the oven for 15-20 minutes.

Eat hot or cold. I serve this salad without a dressing, but if you would prefer to have one it is delicious with a lemon vinaigrette (see page 24) or garlic and rosemary-thyme salad dressing (see page 92).

Quick radish pickles

This is a fantastic pickle to go with salads, soups and main meals. It's ready to eat within 30 minutes of making it, but I usually try to allow three or four hours to let the flavours develop. They will keep in the fridge for a month.

This is nice with thinly sliced carrots and turnip, too.

12 large radishes, very thinly sliced

236ml (8fl.oz/1 cup) cider or white wine vinegar

236ml (8fl.oz/1 cup) water

2 tsp salt

2 tbsp maple syrup or agave, for a sweeter pickle brine (optional)

**OPTIONAL EXTRAS –
ANY OR ALL OF THESE**

½ tsp red pepper flakes (1 tsp for a very spicy pickle)

2 garlic cloves, thinly sliced

1 tsp mustard seeds

1 tsp fennel seeds

1 tsp cumin seeds

1 tsp black peppercorns

Glass preserving jars with lids

Slice the radishes. Cut off the top and bottom, then thinly slice using a mandolin, food processor or sharp knife.

Layer the radish slices in the jar with any of the optional extras that you are using.

Heat the vinegar, water and salt in a pan with the sweetener (if using). Bring to the boil and then simmer for two minutes.

Carefully pour over the pickles in the jar. Replace the lids and leave to cool.

Green tomato and cucumber salad

Green tomatoes are surprisingly delicious raw, especially when allowed to marinade as in this recipe. It is a beautiful colour and smells fantastic too.

4 green tomatoes, cut in half and thinly sliced

1 cucumber, thinly sliced

4 spring onions, thinly sliced

2 cloves garlic, minced

1 tbsp infused lemongrass vinegar (or lime or lemon juice)

3 tbsp olive oil

1 tbsp parsley, finely chopped

1 tbsp lemon or lime basil, finely chopped

Salt and pepper to taste

Make the dressing by whisking together the infused vinegar, oil, garlic and herbs, reserving a little of the chopped herbs to sprinkle on top for serving. Season to taste.

Pour over the tomatoes, cucumbers and onions and stir. Sprinkle the herbs on top and leave in a cool place for 2-3 hours to allow the flavours to develop.

VARIATIONS

Use lemon verbena or lemon balm infused vinegar.

Replace the basil with lemon verbena or lemon balm, or mint.

Replace the parsley with French tarragon or coriander.

Roast autumn fruit, beetroot and calabrese salad

This fruity salad is delicious served on top of couscous or quinoa, with potato wedges, or a salad and crusty bread.

12 plums, halved and stones removed

2 pears, cored and cut into quarters

2 red onions, cut into eighths

2 apples, cored and cut into quarters

2 medium beetroot, peeled and diced

1 head calabrese, cut into florets

Olive oil for roasting

Salt and pepper to taste

2 tbsp blackcurrant balsamic vinegar

6 tbsp olive oil

Fresh basil or French tarragon, chopped

Salad leaves to serve

Preheat the oven to 180°C fan (200°C/400°F/gas mark 6).

Place the beetroot, calabrese and onions on an ovenproof dish, drizzle with oil to evenly coat and put in the oven for 30 minutes.

Meanwhile, prepare the fruit. After 15 minutes, add the fruit to the beetroot and onions and return to the oven for the last 15 minutes.

To prepare the dressing, mix together the vinegar and oil.

Remove the oven dish. If you are eating the salad warm, drizzle with the dressing, sprinkle on some herbs and serve now.

Alternatively, allow to cool and transfer to a serving dish. Drizzle some dressing on top and a generous sprinkle of fresh herbs.

Serve with any leftover dressing.

Sugar free rhubarb relish

I make this relish using no added sugar. The dried fruits, orange and spices cut through the tartness of the rhubarb. I love it as a side with salad, to dip chips in, in sandwiches, served with curries and stirred into gravies.

It is best made a few hours before you want to eat it, to allow the flavours to develop. The relish keeps well for a week or so in the fridge.

500g (17½oz) rhubarb, chopped into 3cm pieces

2 oranges, juice and zest

2 red or white onions, chopped

175g (6oz/1 cup) dates, chopped (or whole sultanas or raisins)

1 tsp fresh ginger, finely chopped

1 tsp ground cinnamon

4 cardamom pods

150ml (5¼fl.oz/⅔ cup) cider or wine vinegar (red or white)

1 chilli, finely chopped (optional)

1 tbsp oil

Pour the oil into a pan and add the onions. Sauté until the onions are soft. Add the rhubarb, orange juice and zest, dried fruit, spices and vinegar and bring to the boil.

Reduce the heat and simmer, stirring occasionally, for 30 minutes.

Allow to cool and transfer into clean jars.

winter seasonal salads

Home preserved bean and tomato salad

This salad is a huge favourite on our courses, especially during the winter when it is rather lovely to be eating summer grown and home saved beans and tomatoes.

We use our dehydrated tomatoes and dried beans, harvested in late summer and stored in large glass jars. Store bought sun-dried tomatoes will be lovely too. If you buy the tomatoes that are stored in oil, you can use that if you wish to make the salad dressing, in place of the olive oil. The salad is delicious with canned beans too.

240g (8½oz/1½ cups) cooked borlotti beans (or other beans of your choice)

55g (2oz/1 cup) dried tomatoes, rehydrated with a little hot water to soften

270g (9½oz/2 cups) red onions, cut in half and sliced

2-4 cloves garlic, sliced

3 tbsp olive oil plus 1 tbsp for cooking the onions

1 tbsp balsamic vinegar

Salt and pepper to taste

Mixed seasonal salad leaves or spinach

Mix the vinegar and oil together, season as you wish.

Pour 1 tbsp oil into a frying pan and add the red onions and garlic. Sauté for 20 minutes until the onions are soft and transparent. Remove from the heat and add the beans and tomatoes (including any soaking liquid). Pour over the dressing and leave to cool.

Chop the salad leaves into a large bowl. Add the cooled bean mixture and stir.

This salad is great to take as a packed lunch, with a chunk of bread to soak up the juices.

Quick summer vegetable pickles

This is so easily made with a cup measure, simply scooping everything up and pouring it into the jar. Adapt this recipe according to what you have on hand. Just make sure you have three cups of vegetables to the brine.

If you do not have cup measures, use a traditional tea cup. It will be fine.

3 cups vegetables – cucumber, Florence fennel, sugar peas, carrot, apple, courgette, summer squash, finely chopped

1 cup cider or white wine vinegar

1 cup water

2 tsp salt

4 tbsp dill or mint, finely chopped

2 tbsp maple syrup or agave, for a sweeter pickle brine (optional)

Glass preserving jars with lids

Layer the vegetables in the jars with the herbs.

Heat the vinegar, water and salt in a pan with the sweetener (if using). Bring to the boil and then simmer for two minutes.

Carefully pour over the pickles in the jar. Replace the lids and leave to cool.

This is ready to eat when cool but is best left for 3-4 hours to allow the flavours to infuse.

'Virgin mojito' cucumber pickles

These are halfway between a salted cucumber and a pickle. They keep their crunchy bite for at least 24 hours so it is worth making plenty for snacking on. They are tasty in a sandwich too.

2 cucumbers

3 limes, juice

A handful fresh mint – I used ginger mint, chopped

2 tbsp white wine vinegar (or cider vinegar)

½ tsp sea salt

Peel the cucumbers (if you wish: older cucumbers can have tough skins but freshly picked are more tender) and slice. Put in a bowl with the lime juice and vinegar.

Sprinkle over the salt – I used a soft grey sea salt and crushed it with my fingers; or use a salt grinder or pestle and mortar – and stir to coat the cucumbers with the liquid.

Put in the fridge or a cool place for 3-4 hours before eating.

If you fancy something a little stronger for a party snack, replace the vinegar with 2 tbsp (or more!) of white rum and reduce the salt to ¼ tsp if you are going to drink the lime-rum liquid afterwards (or use it to make a salad dressing).

Simple salted cucumbers with summer herbs

Despite my best intentions, after the first couple of months of cherishing every one harvested, I always end up with a crazy glut of cucumbers. I seem to make this dish every morning: crunchy, fresh and just enough saltiness, they fly out of the fridge!

1 cucumber

Salt

1 tbsp dill/mint/French tarragon/lemon verbena/basil, finely chopped

Some cucumbers need peeling, some don't. If yours has a thickish skin, then peeling is a good idea.

Slice the cucumber into thick circles. Place in a dish and sprinkle with salt. I usually use 2-3 pinches of sea salt.

Add the herbs and stir. Leave for an hour in a cool place.

Drain the liquid and serve. Try not to eat them all yourself, they really are that good.

roasted 'slugs'

Roasted 'slugs'

This sounds like every gardener's nightmare – roasted slugs with your dinner?! The name came about when I was experimenting with different ways to use up the cucumber glut. These roasted cucumbers are so delicious but they do look a little like slugs …

Honestly, they are lovely.

See also infused cucumber drinks in Chapter 5.

2 cucumbers, peeled if necessary

4 tbsp olive oil

1 tbsp cider or wine vinegar

1 tbsp dill, mint, parsley or basil, finely chopped – plus extra to serve

4 spring onions, sliced

Salt and pepper to taste

Preheat the oven to 180°C fan (200°C/400°F/gas mark 6).

Cut the cucumbers into 6cm lengths. Cut these in half lengthways and then each half into thirds.

Place in a baking tray with the spring onions. Drizzle over 1 tbsp olive oil, season and roast for 30 minutes.

Meanwhile, make the dressing. Mix together 3 tbsp oil, 1 tbsp vinegar and the herbs.

When the cucumbers are cooked, remove from the oven, pour over the dressing and leave to cool.

Place with all of the juices into a serving dish – the juices are lovely to dip bread into. Sprinkle with fresh herbs.

Florence fennel and orange salad

This fresh tasting salad is especially delicious served with bitter leaves where the sweetness of the salad cuts through and compliments the bitterness of the leaves: chicories, radicchio, endive, forced dandelions. Alternatively, use any seasonal salad leaves.

If you can get them, this looks especially striking made with blood oranges.

1 bulb fennel, cut in half lengthways and finely sliced

2 oranges, peeled, cut into quarters and sliced

1 red onion, cut in half and thinly sliced (optional)

60g (2oz/½ cup) nuts – your choice: almonds, walnuts, hazelnuts, pinenuts, etc.

MINT DRESSING

3 tbsp olive oil

1 tbsp white wine vinegar

1 tbsp mint, finely chopped

Salt and pepper to taste

Whisk together the dressing ingredients to combine.

Prepare the fennel, orange and onion using a sharp knife or mandolin.

If you want toasted nuts, spread the nuts on an ovenproof dish and bake at 180°C for 2-3 minutes, shaking the pan to make sure they don't burn. Allow to cool. Alternatively, use raw nuts.

Crush the nuts slightly with a rolling pin to break into smaller pieces.

Put all of the salad ingredients in a bowl, pour over the dressing and combine.

To serve, place the salad leaves (if using) on a dish and arrange the fennel salad on top.

Celery waldorf-ish salad

3 stalks celery, sliced

2 apples, cored and diced

1 cup walnuts

60g (2oz/½ cup) sultanas

DRESSING

70g (2½oz/½ cup) cashews

70g (2½oz/½ cup) sunflower seeds

Hot water

1 tsp cider vinegar or lemon juice

1 tbsp parsley, chopped (plus more to serve)

Salt and pepper to taste

Make the dressing. Soak the cashews and sunflower seeds in hot water for 30 minutes. Drain, reserving the liquid.

Put the nuts, cider vinegar, parsley, seasoning and ¼ cup of the water in a blender and process until smooth and creamy, adding a little more water if necessary.

Place the salad ingredients in a bowl, pour over the dressing and stir. Serve sprinkled with parsley.

Store in the fridge for a week.

VARIATIONS

Replace the walnuts with cashews, hazelnuts, almonds or seeds.

Replace the apples with chopped pear.

Broad bean salad with lemon and mint

500g (17½oz/4 cups) broad beans – podded (this is the weight of the shelled beans, not the pods)

6 tbsp olive oil

1 lemon, juice and zest

2 tbsp fresh mint leaves, finely chopped, plus some whole ones to decorate

Salt and pepper to taste

Whisk the olive oil, lemon juice and zest, mint and seasoning together.

Bring a pan of water to the boil, add the beans and cook for four minutes until tender. Drain, put in a bowl and pour over the dressing. Leave to cool.

Sprinkle with some whole mint leaves to serve.

VARIATIONS

Use raw baby broad beans rather than cooked.

Replace the mint with lemon balm, lemon verbena or French tarragon.

Replace half or all of the broad beans with fresh peas, mangetout or sugar peas.

Summer broad bean salad

200g (7oz/1⅔ cups) broad beans (this is the weight of the shelled beans, not the pods)

200g (7oz/1⅔ cups) tomatoes, diced

200g (7oz/1⅔ cups) cucumber, diced

3 spring onions, thinly sliced (or one small red onion)

3 tbsp olive oil

1 tbsp lemon juice or cider or wine vinegar

Salt and pepper to taste

2 tbsp herbs – e.g. mint, basil, French tarragon, lemon balm, finely chopped
or
2 tbsp coriander, finely chopped

1 chilli, deseeded and finely chopped

1 tsp Za'atar spice mix (see page 22)

Bring a pan of water to the boil, add the beans and cook for four minutes until tender. Drain and cool quickly by running under a cold tap or plunging into a bowl of iced water.

Prepare the salad dressing: place the olive oil, lemon juice or vinegar, seasoning and either option of herbs into a bowl and whisk together to emulsify.

When the beans are cool, put in a mixing bowl with the tomatoes, cucumber and onions. Pour over the dressing, mix and serve.

VARIATION

Replace half or all of the broad beans with fresh peas, mangetout or sugar peas.

Roasted winter vegetable salad with roast garlic and rosemary-thyme dressing

When making a roasted salad, I usually fill the oven with trays of vegetables to make full use of the space. The roasted veg will keep for several days and is so versatile as a base ingredient for soups, stews, pâtés, curries and other dishes. It also freezes very well.

The salad can be eaten hot or cold. It is extremely popular on our courses, the jewel-like colours are enough to entice in the grey of winter. It is very delicious served as it is, with no dressing, too.

Rosemary and thyme are usually available growing outside year round in the garden. The recipe here produces enough dressing for this salad and to use on other meals too. It will keep for a week or so in a jar in the fridge.

The actual quantities of vegetables do not matter too much, I try to have more or less equal quantities of everything. For this recipe I have suggested 125g (4oz/1 cup) of everything, but do experiment and adapt it to suit what you have in your kitchen.

125g (4oz/1 cup) winter squash, diced, peeled if necessary

125g (4oz/1 cup) yellow beetroot, diced

125g (4oz/1 cup) carrots, diced

125g (4oz/1 cup) onions, diced

125g (4oz/1 cup) parsnips, diced

125g (4oz/1 cup) leeks, diced

125g (4oz/1 cup) cabbage, diced

1 cup celeriac, diced

Olive oil to drizzle

Optional – 1 cup cooked borlotti or other beans, nuts or seeds

ROAST GARLIC AND ROSEMARY-THYME DRESSING

1 bulb garlic (or two if you love garlic)

1 tbsp rosemary leaves, finely chopped

1 tbsp thyme leaves, finely chopped

180ml (6fl.oz/¾ cup) olive oil

60ml (2fl.oz/¼ cup) cider vinegar
(or white wine vinegar, or lemon juice)

Salt and pepper to taste

Preheat the oven to 180°C fan (200°C/400°F/gas mark 6).

Arrange the vegetables and the garlic on ovenproof dishes and drizzle with olive oil. Use your fingers or a brush to make sure that everything is evenly coated. Roast for 30 minutes.

Meanwhile, prepare the dressing in readiness for the roasted garlic by mixing the ingredients together.

When the vegetables are cooked, leave to cool; remove the roasted garlic and put in a very cool place to speed up the cooling process.

When the garlic is cool enough to handle comfortably, squeeze the roasted contents out of each clove into the dressing. Whisk thoroughly to combine.

Put the roasted veg into a serving bowl. Add the beans, seeds or nuts (if using) and drizzle over some of the dressing. Stir so that everything is lightly coated, adding a little more dressing if required.

Roasted summer vegetable salad with roast garlic and basil dressing

As with the winter salad, I make as much of this as possible to provide several meals. Vary the ingredients according to what you have in your kitchen and garden.

This salad is a fantastic base for many meals. I love it served with couscous and the Harissa style dressing (see page 120).

As all of the vegetables have slightly different weights, I have approximated here to make it easier for you to replace the ingredients with whatever you have in your kitchen.

125g (4oz/1 cup) aubergine, diced

125g (4oz/1 cup) sweet pepper, diced

125g (4oz/1 cup) courgette or summer squash, diced

125g (4oz/1 cup) cherry tomatoes, halved (or larger tomatoes, quartered)

125g (4oz/1 cup) Chioggia, white or yellow beetroot, diced

125g (4oz/1 cup) turnips, diced

125g (4oz/1 cup) radish, diced

125g (4oz/1 cup) onions, diced (or spring onions, sliced)

125g (4oz/1 cup) cabbage, diced

Olive oil to drizzle

Optional – 1 cup cooked borlotti or other beans, nuts or seeds

ROAST GARLIC AND BASIL DRESSING

1 bulb garlic (or two if you love garlic)

2 tbsp basil, finely chopped

180ml (6fl.oz/¾ cup) olive oil

60ml (2fl.oz/¼ cup) cider vinegar (or white wine vinegar, or lemon juice)

Salt and pepper to taste

Preheat the oven to 180°C fan (200°C/400°F/gas mark 6).

Arrange the vegetables and the garlic on ovenproof dishes and drizzle with olive oil. Use your fingers or a brush to make sure that everything is evenly coated. Roast for 30 minutes.

Meanwhile, prepare the dressing in readiness for the roasted garlic by mixing the ingredients together.

When the vegetables are cooked, leave to cool, remove the roasted garlic and put in a very cool place to speed up the cooling process.

When the garlic is cool enough to handle comfortably, squeeze the roasted contents out of each clove into the dressing. Whisk thoroughly to combine.

Put the roasted veg into a serving bowl. Add the beans, seeds or nuts (if using) and drizzle over some of the dressing. Stir so that everything is lightly coated, adding a little more dressing if required.

Gooseberry salad

I love eating gooseberries fresh from the bush, but some people find them a little tart and so I have included the option of a little extra sweetness in the salad dressing.

300g (10½oz) gooseberries, halved

2 courgettes or summer squash

2 carrots

200g peas, broad beans, sugar peas or mangetout

3 tbsp olive oil

1 tbsp lemon juice or vinegar (cider or wine)

1 tbsp mint or basil

1 tbsp maple syrup, agave or other sweetener (optional)

Bring a pan of water to the boil, add the beans or peas and cook for four minutes until tender. Drain and cool quickly by running under a cold tap or plunging into a bowl of iced water.

Prepare the courgette and carrots by cutting into thin slices or spiralising.

Make the dressing, whisking together the oil, lemon juice or vinegar, herbs and seasoning.

Place all of the vegetables in a mixing bowl, pour over the dressing and mix to coat everything and serve.

Roasted asparagus, radish and spring onion

For a few short weeks we have an abundance of asparagus, at the same time as we are pulling fresh radishes (sown to mark the rows in the parsnip bed) and spring onions.

I like to keep the asparagus and spring onions long; it is rather pleasurable picking them up and eating with your fingers (a knife and fork is fine too, if you prefer!)

500g (17 ½oz) asparagus, tough ends removed

10 medium radishes, sliced

6 fat spring onions, sliced in half lengthways (or 10-12 thin ones, whole)

1 tbsp olive oil for roasting

DRESSING

3 tbsp olive oil

1 tbsp white wine or white balsamic vinegar

1 tbsp lemon juice

1 tbsp herbs – mint, lemon verbena, French tarragon or basil, finely chopped (plus more to decorate)

Salt and pepper to taste

Preheat the oven to 180°C fan (200°C/400°F/gas mark 6).

Arrange the asparagus, radishes and spring onions on a baking tray and drizzle with olive oil. Season with salt if you wish (a homemade herb salt is especially nice here).

Put in the oven and roast for 12-15 minutes, turning once half way through the cooking time.

Remove from the oven and cool.

Whisk together the dressing, season to taste.

Arrange the roasted vegetables on a serving dish. Drizzle over the dressing and sprinkle with herbs.

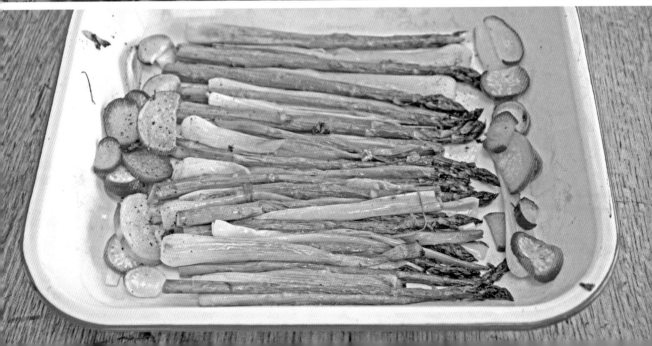

Roasted squash salad with toasted pumpkin seeds

This is especially delicious made using a full flavoured homegrown squash such as Crown Prince, Uchiki Kuri or Marina di Chioggia. I often serve it just as it is, with no dressing, as the taste of roasted squash is so sweet, nutty and delicious.

Sometimes I try out a new variety of squash and am disappointed in the flavour. No matter, I then use a more strongly flavoured dressing drizzled over the top.

I always roast a whole squash regardless of size. On course days, I will usually serve the squash in three different ways: soup, salad and hummus or pâté. It's a useful addition to so many meals, keeps for several days in the fridge and can be frozen.

1 squash, deseeded, peeled if necessary and diced

3 red or white onions, cut into eighths

130g (4½oz/1 cup)

Olive oil for roasting

Salt and pepper to taste

SUGGESTED DRESSINGS

Cashew and orange salad page 24

Lemon vinaigrette page 24

Orange vinaigrette page 62

Tahini dressing page 61

VARIATIONS

Replace the squash with roasted turnip, parsnip or celeriac.

Replace the pumpkin seeds with sunflower seeds or nuts.

Preheat the oven to 180°C fan (200°C/400°F/gas mark 6).

Prepare the vegetables and arrange on an ovenproof dish. Drizzle olive oil over and make sure everything is lightly coated, using your fingers or a brush. Roast in the oven for 25-30 minutes and allow to cool.

Spread the pumpkin seeds over a baking tray and cook for 2-3 minutes, shaking occasionally so that the seeds do not burn. Leave to cool.

Put the roasted vegetables in a dish, sprinkle over the seeds and season if you wish.

Serve as it is to fully enjoy the flavour of your squash, or with a dressing.

Spinach, roast squash and spiced chickpeas

Mix up the greens in this salad with whatever you have in the kitchen or garden: spinach, kale, chard, mustards, mixes salad leaves, spring greens, shredded cabbage.

This makes a tasty packed lunch in a jar and is also delicious served hot. I like it with potato wedges, seasoned with some homemade herb salt and smoked paprika. You can cook these in the oven at the same time.

500g (17½oz) squash, diced

2 tbsp olive oil

240g (8½oz/1½ cups) chickpeas
(or cooked broad beans, other beans
or carlin peas)

3 tsp Za'atar style seasoning (see page 22)

200g (7oz/4 cups) spinach, shredded

Salt and pepper to taste

Preheat the oven to 180°C fan (200°C/400°F/gas mark 6).

Arrange the squash on a baking tray and drizzle 1½ tbsp oil over to coat. Season and cook for 10 minutes, then turn over.

As the squash is cooking, mix the seasoning, ½ tbsp oil and chickpeas in a bowl. Spread over a baking tray.

After turning over the squash, put the chickpeas in the oven and cook both for 15 minutes more. Check the chickpeas every five minutes and turn to make sure they are evenly cooked.

If you are serving this hot, mix the squash, chickpeas and shredded leaves together.

Otherwise, allow the squash and chickpeas to cool before mixing with the leaves.

I like this as it is, but if you want a dressing, it is tasty with the tahini dressing on pages 61 and 118 or a lemon vinaigrette (page 24).

TIP This is about the size of a small squash, if you are using a large one, roast the whole diced squash (you will need more oil) and weigh the 500g when cooked. Reserve the rest of the squash for another recipe.

Seasonal hummus

I make a hummus of some kind for every gardening course lunch at Homeacres, everyone loves the bright colours, especially welcome in the winter months. Add your choice of vegetables, leaves and herbs. It is a good way of using up leftovers in the fridge, too.

VEGETABLE SUGGESTIONS

Cooked – beetroot, squash, parsnip, carrot, onion, swede, sweet peppers, kale, tomatoes, courgette

Raw – spinach, kale, tomatoes, courgette, cucumber

Herbs – parsley, basil, coriander, dill, French tarragon

330g (12oz/2 cups) cooked chickpeas (reserve the cooking liquor)

240g (8½oz/2 cups) vegetables

4 tsp tahini

2 or 3 cloves garlic, chopped

1 lemon, juice (3½ tsp)

½ tsp freshly ground cumin seed

½ tsp ground coriander

2 tbsp olive oil

2 tbsp seasonal herbs, chopped

Salt and pepper to taste

Add everything except the cooking liquid into a food processor. Turn on, gradually drizzling the liquid into the mixture until it is the texture you like.

Cucumber and czar bean hummus

240g (8½oz/1½ cups) cooked czar or other white beans

225g (8oz/1 cup) cucumber, chopped

2 cloves garlic

1 tbsp olive oil

2 tbsp tahini

1 lemon, juice and zest

1 tbsp fresh dill, parsley or mint, chopped (plus more for serving)

Salt and pepper to taste

Place the beans, cucumber, garlic, tahini, herbs and seasoning in a food processor. Blend until smooth.

Transfer to a serving dish and sprinkle with herbs. Drizzle over the olive oil.

VARIATION

Replace the cucumber with courgette or summer squash.

seasonal hummus with roasted squash

roasted beetroot,
carrot and nut hummus

Roast beetroot, carrot and nut hummus

300g (10½oz) beetroot, diced

300g (10½oz) carrot, diced

100g (3½oz) almonds (hazelnuts or walnuts)

Olive oil

1 tbsp parsley or coriander, finely chopped (plus more to decorate)

1 tsp ground cumin

1 tsp ground coriander

1 clove garlic, finely chopped

A little water

Salt and pepper to taste

VARIATIONS

Replace the roasted beetroot and/ or carrot with roasted squash, leek, parsnip or celeriac.

Preheat the oven to 180°C fan (200°C/400°F/gas mark 6).

Arrange the beetroot and carrots on a baking tray and drizzle with oil, using a brush or your fingers to make sure that everything is coated.

Roast for 20 minutes until the vegetables are soft.

Spread the nuts on a baking tray and roast for 3-4 minutes, so that they are toasted. Check the pan and shake several times to ensure that they cook evenly and don't get burned. (Alternatively, you can add the nuts uncooked.)

Place the roasted veg, nuts, spices, garlic and chopped herbs in a food processor and blend to make a smooth paste. Add a little water if necessary. Season to taste.

Transfer into a serving bowl and sprinkle with chopped fresh herbs.

Roast beetroot and borlotti bean hummus

This is delicious made with red or golden beetroot. The lighter coloured beetroots are still tasty but give the hummus a paler colour. You can use boiled beetroot if you prefer.

450g (16oz) beetroot, diced

240g (8½oz/1½ cups) cooked borlotti beans

Olive oil to roast

1 lemon, juice and zest

1 tbsp finely chopped parsley or coriander (plus more to decorate)

1 tsp ground cumin

1 tsp ground coriander

1 clove garlic, finely chopped

A little water

Salt and pepper to taste

Preheat the oven to 180°C fan (200°C/400°F/gas mark 6).

Arrange the beetroot on a baking tray and drizzle with oil, using a brush or your fingers to make sure that everything is coated.

Roast for 20 minutes until the beetroot is soft.

Place the roasted beetroot, lemon juice and zest, spices, garlic and chopped herbs in a food processor and blend to make a smooth paste. Add a little water if necessary. Season to taste.

Transfer into a serving bowl and sprinkle with chopped fresh herbs.

VARIATIONS

Replace the roasted beetroot with roasted squash, leek, carrot, courgette, onion, parsnip or celeriac.

Replace the borlotti beans with other dried beans, broad beans or peas.

Sun-dried tomato and bean pâté

This is a great store cupboard pâté that takes just a few minutes to put together. I use home-dehydrated tomatoes, but bought sun dried will be delicious too. If you use the kind that comes in jars of oil, reduce the olive oil in this recipe.

The flavour will vary according to the beans you use, alternatively replace the beans with cooked chickpeas or peas such as carlin.

Add more soaking water (or plain water) to make a creamy dip for vegetables.

400g (15oz/1½ cups) cooked beans
(e.g. czar, borlotti, kidney, canellini)

30g (1oz/½ cup) dried tomatoes

½ lemon, juice

2-3 cloves garlic, chopped

2-3 tbsp olive oil

A little hot water (for the dried tomatoes)

3 tbsp fresh basil (when not in season, substitute with parsley) plus extra to sprinkle

1 tsp oregano, chopped (or thyme leaves)

Salt and pepper to taste

Chop the tomatoes and put in a bowl. Add enough hot water to just cover and leave for 10 minutes. Drain, reserving the soaking liquid.

Put the beans, tomatoes, herbs and lemon juice, with a few grindings of black pepper, a pinch of salt and 2 tbsp of olive oil in the food processor.

Blend, adding a little of the soaking liquid until the pâté is the consistency you like. Taste and season further if you wish.

Sprinkle with some more fresh chopped herbs to serve.

TIP   For an oil free version, replace the olive oil with 2-3 tbsp of soaking liquid or water.

Borlotti bean, pumpkin seed and walnut pâté

A luxurious tasting pâté, this also makes a tasty stuffing for baked tomatoes, summer squash, small winter squash or peppers. You can replace the herbs with your choice of mint, dill, chervil or French tarragon.

240g (8½oz/1½ cups) cooked borlotti beans (or red kidney beans)

100g (3½oz/1 cup) walnuts, lightly toasted

130g (4½oz/1 cup) pumpkin seeds, lightly toasted

1-3 cloves garlic, minced

1 tsp smoked paprika

1 tsp thyme, chopped

1 tbsp parsley, chopped

1 tbsp chives, chopped

1 tbsp summer savoury, chopped

2 tbsp olive oil

Water to mix

Salt and pepper to taste

Place all of the ingredients except the water in a food processor. Blend, slowly adding a little water, until it is the texture you like.

Serve with a drizzle of olive oil on top and a sprinkle of freshly chopped herbs.

TIP   Red wine salt is very good in this, and sprinkled over the top.

Aubergine, courgette and onion baba ganoush

This is my simplified version of the classic smokey dish, another way of using up courgettes during the summer abundance. Roasting the vegetables imparts a sweet depth of flavour, not the smokiness of the traditional way of preparing aubergines for baba ganoush, by grilling them whole, but this way is quicker.

This is velvety and very moreish.

500g (17½oz) aubergine

250g (8¾oz) courgette

250g (8¾oz) onions

1 lemon, juice and zest

3 tbsp tahini

½ tsp red pepper flakes
(sweet or hot, according to taste)

1 tsp ground cumin

½ tsp smoked paprika (or more if you like)

Salt and pepper to taste

Roast small aubergine whole, larger ones cut into halves or quarters. Slice the courgettes in half and the onions into quarters. Drizzle with olive oil and roast for about 25 minutes. Leave to cool.

Peel the aubergines and discard the skins into the compost.

Place all of the ingredients into a food processor and blend into a creamy paste.

Serve sprinkled with more smoked paprika or fresh herbs.

White bean, aubergine and onion pâté

A glut of aubergines inspired this pâté, which I first made for one of our course lunches. It's not often that we have a glut of aubergines in England! You can replace the aubergines with other roast vegetables, for example sweet pepper, mushrooms, courgettes or summer squash.

I used czar beans but any white bean is fine, or experiment with other beans or peas.

The aubergine and onions take about 25 minutes to roast (see Aubergine, courgette and onion baba ganoush recipe on the previous page).

240g (8½oz/1½ cups) czar beans

250g (8½oz/2½ cups) aubergine, roasted

250g (8½oz/2 cups) onion, roasted

2-4 cloves garlic

1 lemon, juice

1 tsp ground cumin

1 tbsp fresh basil, chopped

1 tbsp fresh coriander or parsley, chopped

Salt and pepper to taste

A little olive oil or water, if needed

Peel the aubergines (you can leave the skins on, and I do if using the softer skinned green, white and violet aubergines, but the purple skins can be bitter).

Place everything in the food processor and blend into a smooth pâté. If it is a little thick, add some olive oil or water and process until the pâté is the texture you desire.

Seasonal greens, herbs and lime pesto

You can use any greens in this zingy pesto – spinach, kale, chard, mustards, mixed salad leaves, spring greens. It is delicious as a dip, drizzled over salads or mixed through rice, pasta or grains. Refrigerate any leftovers for 3-4 days, or freeze individual portions in an ice tray for later use.

If you do not have (or like) coriander, replace with basil, parsley, dill or mint. The walnuts can be replaced with toasted almonds, hazelnuts, cashews, sunflower or pumpkin seeds. The flavour will be different of course!

2 cups greens, chopped

1 cup coriander, chopped

2-4 cloves garlic, chopped

1 lime, juice (and zest if you want it very lime flavoured)

1 cup walnuts, toasted

¼ cup olive oil
(approximately, you may not need it all)

Salt and pepper to taste

Add the greens, coriander, garlic, walnuts, lime and seasoning to a food processor.

As it is processing, drizzle some olive oil in until the pesto is smooth.

Taste and adjust seasoning, if required.

Cooking intensifies the flavour but if you prefer, the nuts and seeds may be added raw.

Fabulous fennel frond pesto

This is a tasty way of using those beautiful long fennel fronds. I like to use walnuts or hazelnuts in this recipe. This is delicious stirred through pasta or noodles for a quick meal.

2 cloves garlic

100g (3½oz/1 cup) nuts, toasted or raw

50g (1½oz/2¾ cups) fennel fronds, chopped

60ml (2fl.oz/¼ cup) olive oil

1 lemon, juice and zest

Salt and pepper to taste

A little water, if needed

Place all of the ingredients in a food processor and blend until puréed. Stop once or twice to scrape down any escaped fronds with a spatula, to make sure that everything is properly combined. Add a little water if necessary to make a smooth paste.

Country capers

Capers are a tasty addition to salads, dressings and sauces. I make my own country versions using nasturtium seeds or the buds from dandelions, wild garlic and scapes (garlic, onion, leek). You can also add chive blossoms.

1 glass jar with lid and 1 fermenting weight

BASIC CAPER BRINE

1 cup water

½ cup vinegar – white wine, cider, champagne

¼ cup sea salt

EXTRA FLAVOURINGS (OPTIONAL)

Garlic cloves, French tarragon, dill, citrus peels, lemon balm, peppercorns, juniper berries

2 cups 'capers' – make sure they are clean and free from insects

Put the salt, vinegar and water in a pan, bring to the boil and stir until the salt has dissolved. Remove from the heat.

Pack the jar with the 'capers' layered with any additions. Pour over the brine making sure the 'capers' are completely submerged, agitating them with a glass stirrer or similar to remove any air pockets. Add the fermenting weight and replace the lid.

Leave for a week to a month, depending how pickled you like them.

Once opened, keep in the fridge.

4
WHOLE MEALS

This is a selection of wholesome whole meals for filling, nourishing dinners using your homegrown or seasonally bought vegetables. I love experimenting with different cuisines, it is fun adapting the ingredients to suit the produce in my garden, exploring "what can I use instead of …?"

Many of these dishes take longer to prepare than the other recipes in the book but that does allow more time to appreciate the pleasure of making something delicious from seasonal vegetables.

Unless otherwise stated, each of the following recipes is designed to feed four hungry people.

Aubergine layered 'lasagne'

This hearty lasagne is delicious cold with salad the next day, if there is any left.

600g (21oz) aubergines

500g (17½oz/3½ cups) onions, diced

3 cloves garlic

2 stalks celery, diced

600g (21oz) courgettes

1 red pepper, diced

100g (3½oz/2 cups) spinach or chard, chopped

Olive oil

800g (28oz/5⅓ cup) tomatoes, chopped

Plus 2 or 3 tomatoes, sliced, to decorate

240g (8½oz/1½ cups) cooked beans (400g tin, drained)

1-2 tbsp chopped herbs – basil, parsley or oregano (or a mixture of all three)

Salt and pepper to taste

FOR THE GARLIC BREAD

A crusty loaf of bread

4-10 cloves garlic (I like it strong!)

½-1 cup olive oil (it depends how large the loaf is)

Pepper

An oven dish approximately 25 x 25cm (10 x 10in)

Preheat the oven to 180°C fan (200°C/400°F/gas mark 6).

Finely chop the garlic and mix into the olive oil. Add a little pepper, stir and leave to infuse.

Slice the aubergines and courgettes lengthways into 5mm thick slices.

Pour some olive oil into the pan and soften the onions, garlic and celery on a low heat.

When cooked, add the red pepper, beans and tomatoes. Simmer for around 15 minutes until the sauce is cooked through.

Meanwhile, drizzle olive oil onto a griddle and cook the aubergines and courgettes, several slices at a time, turning occasionally, for 3-4 minutes.

Pour some of the tomato sauce into the oven dish, add a layer of aubergine, then more sauce, a layer of courgette, and so on until the dish is filled with layers of sauce, aubergine and courgette. Decorate with slices of tomato.

Put in the oven and bake for 30 minutes.

Slice the bread so the knife goes about 90% through the loaf, leaving the base intact and the slices attached to each other. Put in a baking dish and, using a spoon, drizzle the garlic oil over both sides of each slice.

15 minutes before the lasagne is ready, put the bread in the oven.

When the lasagne is cooked, remove from the oven and serve with the crusty garlic bread and a large salad, or dish of steamed seasonal green vegetables.

TIP   A frying pan will work if you don't have a griddle.

This recipe adapts well to other vegetables. In the winter, use slices of cooked potato, parsnip, sweet potato or squash. Cooked whole cabbage and kale leaves make lovely 'lasagne sheets' too.

Bean stew with red wine

Use whatever beans you like for this delicious, rich bean stew. I especially like to use borlotti or the large Greek gigantes. This casserole is so simple to prepare yet the complexity and depth of flavours makes it a feast in a casserole dish.

For a complete meal in a pot, use parsnip or potatoes along with the kohl rabi. Puréed leftovers make a lovely soup which freezes well.

280g (10oz/2 cups) onions, chopped

170g (6oz/1½ cups) (2 stalks) celery, sliced

2-4 garlic cloves (more if you like it), minced

600g (21oz/4 cups) tomatoes, diced

300g (10oz/2 cups) carrots, sliced

480g (16½oz/3 cups) cooked beans
(2 tins, drained)

1 tsp thyme, chopped

1 tsp rosemary, chopped

1 tbsp parsley, chopped

½-1 tsp smoked paprika

250g (9oz/2½ cups) leeks, sliced

125g (1½oz/3½ cups) green leaves,
shredded (kale, spinach, spring cabbage,
chard – whatever is in season)

500g (17½oz/3½ cups) kohl rabi, diced
(or celeriac, parsnip, potato, turnip, swede)

500ml (17fl.oz/2¼ cups) red wine or stock,
or half and half

1 tbsp olive oil

Salt and pepper to taste

A large pan or casserole dish

Pour the oil into the pan and sauté the onions, leek, celery and garlic until soft.

Add the carrots, herbs, beans, kohl rabi, leaves and stir to coat with oil.

Add the tomatoes, smoked paprika, seasoning and red wine (or stock).

Bring to the boil, turn the heat down and simmer with the lid on for 45 minutes.

Serve with fresh vegetables, mashed potatoes, rice or crusty bread.

Leek and czar bean savoury crumble

This is a warm, filling and nurturing dish, ideal for cold days. A complete meal in itself, I like to serve it with more vegetables from the allotment – Brussel sprouts, carrots, radicchio, cabbage or kale.

If you prefer, replace the crumble topping with mashed potato and swede; the cooking time will be the same.

In the summer, when leeks are not in season, replace them with 500g of summer vegetables – e.g. courgettes, sweet peppers, aubergines, summer squash.

I like to use yellow pea flour to make the crumble; regular wheat flour is tasty too.

210g (7oz/1½ cups) onion, diced

500g (17½oz/5 cups) leeks, trimmed and cut into 2.5cm/1in slices

2 cloves garlic, minced

280g (8½oz/1½ cups) butter beans (2 tins, drained)

70g (2½oz/2 cups) leafy greens, chopped (kale, chard, spinach)

1 tbsp fresh parsley or French tarragon, chopped

½ tsp sage, chopped

400ml (13½fl.oz/1⅔ cups) vegetable stock

1 tbsp olive oil

Salt and pepper to taste

FOR THE CRUMBLE TOPPING

115g (4oz/1¼ cups) chickpea or pea flour

85g (3oz/1 cup) oats

60g (2oz/½ cup) nuts or seeds, chopped

60g (2oz/¼ cup) olive oil – plus more if needed

½ tsp rosemary leaves, chopped

½ tsp thyme leaves, chopped

1 tsp parsley, chopped

Salt and pepper to taste

Preheat the oven to 180°C fan (200°C/400°F/gas mark 6).

In an oven and hob proof dish, soften the onion, garlic and leeks in the olive oil until transparent. Add the greens and stir, then add the beans, stock (with wine if using) and herbs. Cook for five minutes.

Place the oats, flour, nuts (or seeds), seasoning and herbs in a bowl. Pour over ¼ cup of the oil and stir to combine. Mix with your fingers to make a mixture that resembles breadcrumbs, adding a little more oil if it feels too dry.

Remove the leek and bean mixture from the heat, pour the crumble over and bake in the oven for 30 minutes. Remove from the oven and serve.

I often prepare the vegetables and roast them alongside the crumble, to save fuel.

If you don't have an oven and hob proof dish, cook the filling in a pan and then pour into an oven dish before topping with the crumble and baking.

TIP For a festive occasion, replace 250ml of the stock with white wine.

Cooked summer vegetable carpaccio

This recipe takes some time to assemble, so do read the recipe through carefully and plan the various stages. To make most use of the oven's heat, I always cook extra vegetables to make into salads or soup.

There is no need to weigh the vegetables in this dish. If you can, choose one red and one yellow beetroot, for added colour.

2 medium aubergine

2 medium courgette (or summer squash)

2 medium beetroot

2 medium carrots, sliced in half lengthways

Olive oil

FOR THE MARINADE

4 tsp olive oil

1 lemon, juice and zest

2 tsp herbs, finely chopped – parsley, basil, French tarragon, or oregano

FOR THE HERB PESTO

120ml (4fl.oz/½ cup) olive oil

2 cloves garlic (4 if you like garlic!)

40g (1½oz/2 cups) fresh herbs e.g. parsley, basil, French tarragon, or oregano

FOR THE SALSA

6 medium tomatoes, diced

3 spring onions, thinly sliced

2 cloves garlic

1 chilli (optional)

1 lime, juice

FOR THE GARLIC TAHINI DRESSING

240g (8½oz/1 cup) tahini

1 lemon, juice and zest

2 cloves garlic, minced

150ml (5fl.oz/½ cup) water, as needed

A pinch of sea salt

Preheat the oven to 180°C fan (200°C/400°F/gas mark 6).

Two hours (at least) before making the meal, place the washed but unpeeled beetroot in an oven dish and bake until soft. This usually takes around an hour. After 40 minutes, add the carrots to the dish, drizzle over some olive oil and return to the oven for 20 minutes until cooked. Check they are soft with a sharp knife or skewer.

Remove from the oven and allow to cool.

Peel the beetroot and slice into 3-5mm slices, using a knife or mandolin.

Whilst the beetroot is cooking and cooling, make the marinade by whisking the ingredients together in a jug.

Slice the aubergine and courgette into 3-5mm slices and place in a dish with the marinade. Leave on one side for 15 minutes, using this time to make the other dressings.

The pesto – blend the ingredients together using an immersion blender or food processor.

The tahini dressing – put the tahini, lemon, garlic and pinch of salt in a bowl. Gradually mix in the water, whisking together until it has the consistency of thick cream. You may need to add a little extra water.

The salsa – finely chop the garlic and chilli (if using) and mix with the ingredients in a bowl.

When the aubergine etc. have marinated, heat a griddle and drizzle with olive oil. Carefully griddle the aubergine and courgette several slices at a time, turning occasionally, until they are cooked through. Leave to cool.

When all of the vegetables are cool, assemble your dish. Drizzle tahini dressing over the slices of beetroot and the carrots and pesto over the courgette and aubergine. There will be leftover sauces for serving

Serve: with the salsa and extra pesto and tahini, with a salad of seasonal leaves and flat breads, pitta breads, couscous or rice.

WINTER VARIATION

Replace the vegetables with roasted winter root vegetables: parsnips, carrots, winter squash, celeriac etc.

Seasonal vegetable couscous with harissa style dressing

This recipe welcomes whatever vegetables you have, it is very much a 'use what you have in the kitchen (allotment or bargain bin at the supermarket)' meal, the main ingredients varying with the seasons.

I usually don't weigh the veg at all for this, but cook enough to fill my pan or prepare two large trays of whatever I have and roast them. I have given an approximate guideline for four people. This dish makes great leftovers; a useful standby to have in the fridge for lunches. It is worth doubling the dressing too!

FOR THE COUSCOUS

500g (17½oz/3⅓ cups) couscous (quinoa for gluten free version)

Water or stock

VEGETABLES

Prepare around 1kg (35oz/7 cups) of vegetables, all chopped to a similar size.

SUMMER VEGETABLES	WINTER VEGETABLES
Courgette	Squash
Summer squash	Swede
Tomatoes	Carrot
Aubergine	Yellow beetroot (or other light coloured beetroot)
Salad potatoes	Parsnip
Broad beans	
Peas	Kohl rabi
Florence fennel	Celeriac
Spring cabbage	Cabbage
Turnip	Kale
Sweet peppers	Beetroot
Beetroot	

ADDITIONAL INGREDIENTS

250g (9oz/1½ cups) chickpeas/white beans/almonds or cashews

½ cup raisins, apricots or other dried fruit

Fresh lemon or lime juice

Olive oil

SPICE MIX

½ tbsp fresh ginger, finely chopped

½ tbsp ground coriander

½ tbsp ground cumin

1 tbsp sweet paprika

½ tsp fennel seeds, crushed

½ tsp cinnamon

1 tsp chilli powder or 1-2 red chillies, according to taste

Salt and pepper to taste

Fresh coriander, parsley, mint or basil

FOR THE HARISSA STYLE DRESSING

½ tsp coriander seed

½ tsp cumin seed

½ tsp fennel seed

½ cup sun-dried tomatoes, soaked for 15 minutes and drained (retain the soaking liquid)

225g (8oz/1 cup) cooked tomatoes (canned tomatoes are fine)

1 tsp smoked paprika

1 tbsp fresh mint

1 tbsp fresh coriander

1 tbsp lemon juice

2 tbsp olive oil

2 cloves garlic

1-2 chillies, deseeded (optional)

Water, as necessary

Toast the coriander, cumin and fennel seeds in a hot pan for two minutes, stirring continually so they don't burn.

Remove from heat, cool and grind to a powder.

Put all of the ingredients except the soaking liquid into a food processor. Purée the harissa, gradually adding the soaking liquid and more water if necessary, until everything has been blended and the texture resembles thick cream.

Sauté the onion and garlic in the olive oil.

Add the herb and spice mix, stir, then add the chopped vegetables and stir to coat everything with the oil. If you are using nuts, add these now too. Pour water or stock to cover the vegetables, bring to the boil then reduce heat to a simmer.

With the lid on, cook for 20 minutes.

After 15 minutes, add the beans and raisins.

Stir and add a little extra (boiling) water if it looks a bit dry.

Alternatively, roast the vegetables in the oven.

Make the couscous according to the packet instructions (they vary according to the size and type of couscous) then carefully stir with a fork to fluff it up.

Place the couscous in a warm serving dish, then add the vegetable mixture. Sprinkle fresh herbs on the top.

Serve with the harissa style dressing. Tahini dressing (pages 61 and 118) is also delicious with this.

Any leftovers make a lovely cold salad, or stuffing for a squash.

The harissa style dressing keeps for about two weeks in the fridge.

Baked aubergine and courgette skewers

I find baking easier than grilling these skewers as they are less likely to stick, but this recipe can be used under the grill, or on a griddle or a barbecue if you prefer. The quantity of skewers depends on their size.

2 medium aubergines

2 medium courgettes

2 medium carrots

250g cherry tomatoes

250g small onions or shallots, peeled

(Other possible vegetables – mushrooms, 1 inch pieces of sweet potato or chunks of squash)

MARINADE

4 tbsp pomegranate molasses
(or maple syrup/agave)

1 lemon, juice and zest

4 cloves garlic, minced

½ tsp smoked paprika

½ tsp chilli powder

½ tsp cinnamon

4 tbsp olive oil

10-12 skewers

A large ovenproof tray

Preheat the oven to 180°C fan (200°C/400°F/gas mark 6).

Slice the aubergines, carrots and courgettes lengthways into 5mm slices. Place in a dish with the marinade, stir to coat and leave for at least 30 minutes.

Fill a small bowl with water, adding a slice of lemon or sprig of mint and place a clean towel ready. This is for your fingers, it is a sticky job!

Thread the vegetables onto the skewers by folding into a Z shape, alternating with the whole cherry tomatoes and onions. Place each one in the tray. When all of the vegetables have been skewered, brush with the marinade and place in the oven.

Cook for 25-30 minutes.

Serve hot with:

Seasonal greens, herbs and lime pesto (see page 109)

Tahini dressing (see pages 61 and 118)

Simple tomato salsa (see page 118)

Warmed pitta breads

Seasonal greens and aubergine dhal

Delicious and filling, you can easily adapt this recipe for the winter and spring, or for those who do not like aubergine, replace the aubergine with mushrooms or squash. It makes a lovely filling for pitta breads or wraps too, rather like a kind of dhal 'burrito' with salad and pickles.

200g (7oz/1 cup) lentils, red or green

1-2 tbsp sunflower oil plus more as needed

450g (16oz/4 cups) aubergine, diced

300g (6oz) seasonal greens – kale, cabbage, spinach, beetroot leaves – chopped

150g (5oz/1 cup) tomatoes, chopped (canned tomatoes are fine)

2 onions, sliced

4 cloves garlic, minced

1 tsp fresh ginger, finely chopped

1 tsp ground coriander

1 tsp ground cumin

½ tsp ground cinnamon

1 tbsp garam masala

Salt and pepper to taste

Water or vegetable stock

Small bunch of fresh coriander to serve

Put the lentils in a pan with 600ml (22fl.oz/3 cups) stock or water, bring to the boil, reduce heat and simmer for around 30 minutes until cooked.

Meanwhile, place the onions, ginger and garlic in a large pan with a little sunflower oil and cook until the onion is soft.

Add the spices and stir, then add aubergine and tomatoes.

Simmer until the aubergine is cooked through, adding more oil if necessary, then add the lentils and greens. Stir and simmer for 10 minutes.

Sprinkle with chopped fresh coriander leaves. (If you don't have fresh coriander, parsley and mint are delicious too.)

Serve with poppadoms, quick spiced pickles, tomato and cucumber salad and rice or spiced root vegetables (see overleaf).

Tomato and cucumber salad

2 or 3 tomatoes, diced

1 cucumber, diced

3 spring onions, chopped into 5mm pieces, including some of the green part

¼ cup olive or other light oil

2 cloves garlic

2 tbsp cider vinegar

2 tbsp lime juice

¼ tsp ground cumin

¼ tsp ground coriander

Salt and pepper to taste

1 tbsp fresh coriander, chopped

1 tbsp fresh mint, chopped

First make the dressing: put the oil, garlic, vinegar, lime juice and spices into a bowl and whisk together. Taste and season with salt and pepper.

Add the vegetables and fresh herbs and stir.

Quick spiced pickles

1 tbsp ground sea salt

1 tbsp mustard seeds

1 tbsp fennel seeds

2 cucumber, sliced

1 carrot, thinly sliced

1 tsp chilli powder

½ tsp turmeric

1 lemon, juice, or1 lime, juice

Toast the salt and spice seeds in a heavy pan for a minute or two, shaking the pan to stop them burning. Leave to cool then grind into a powder.

Put everything into a bowl and mix. This can be eaten right away but tastes better if left for the flavours to infuse for three or four hours.

This can be kept refrigerated for a week.

Spiced root vegetables – serve warm or cold

These vegetables will be firm to the bite; cook for a little longer if you prefer them soft.

1 tsp black mustard seeds

1 tsp cumin seeds

1 tsp coriander seeds

1 tsp fennel seeds

1 tsp turmeric

4 cloves garlic, minced

1-2 chillies, finely chopped – more if you like things spicy!

50g (1½oz/1 cup) fresh coriander leaves, chopped (or parsley, mint or a spicy basil such as Thai basil)

Sunflower oil

Water

500g (17½oz/4 cups) of seasonal grated vegetables – choose your own combination of carrot, kohl rabi, parsnip, celeriac, light coloured beetroot, mooli or other radish

Other vegetables that also work well (not roots) summer or winter squash, courgette

Heat a little oil in a large pan or wok and add the spices, garlic and chilli. Stir for two minutes then add the grated vegetables. Stir thoroughly to coat with spices, add 100ml water, stir and cover with a lid.

Simmer for five minutes, stir and serve warm as a companion to a hot dish, or cold as a salad.

This makes a tasty stuffing for squash or peppers and a crunchy sandwich filling with fresh salad leaves and sliced tomatoes.

Parsnip, kale and carrot bhajis

I usually double or triple the quantities here. These bhajis are light and so moreish, they keep well in the fridge for a couple of days and freeze well.

180g (6oz/1 cup) parsnip, grated

180g (8oz/1 cup) carrot, grated

70g (2½oz/1 cup) kale leaves

135g (4¾oz/1 cup) onion

110g (4oz/1 cup) pea flour (yellow or green) or gram flour*

Water to mix

Salt and pepper to taste

2 cloves garlic, finely chopped

3 tsp spices

Sunflower oil

*   See Appendix for suppliers of pea flour

Shred the kale and thinly slice the onion.

Put in a roomy bowl with the parsnip, carrot, green pea flour, garlic, spices, salt and pepper. Stir to combine then add about 120ml (4fl.oz/½ cup) water slowly to make a batter. You may need to add a little more, the amount of liquid will depend on the flour used.

The mixture should be well covered with thick batter which resembles double cream.

In a deep solid pan or wok, heat 2.5cm/1" oil. Drop a little batter or a small cube of bread into the oil to check – if it sizzles, the oil is hot enough.

Using a dessert spoon, add six spoonfuls of mixture to the pan. Use a slotted spoon to turn the bhajis until they are golden and cooked on both sides (around four minutes altogether).

Place on a plate and cook more bhajis until all are done.

Place the bhajis on a clean tea towel or kitchen paper to drain.

Kitchenware for sale in the market, Chiang Mai, Thailand

Summer vegetable curry with spicy basil

This light, creamy curry is a real taste of summer and reminds me of sitting in the village in Thailand where my Dad lives, eating in a tiny café beside the klong (a waterway used for irrigation) enterprisingly set up under a gazebo on the chef's driveway. Her curry is much spicier, do add more chillies if you too like things spicy.

300g (7oz/2 cups) courgette, sliced (or summer squash)

260g (6oz/2 cups) onion, sliced

500g (17½oz/4 cups) vegetables, e.g. cauliflower, broccoli, French beans, sweetcorn

110g (4oz/1 cup) sweet pepper, diced

150g (5oz/1 cup) tomatoes, diced

250g (8½oz) aubergine – long Thai green ones are especially nice here

2-4 cloves garlic, minced

1-2 chillies, finely chopped (deseeded if you want less heat)

450ml (16fl.oz/2 cups) coconut milk

225ml (8fl.oz/1 cup) stock or water

1 tbsp soy sauce

2 stalks lemongrass, cut into 8cm pieces and lightly crushed

25g (1oz/½ cup) coriander leaves

25g (1oz/½ cup) coriander stems and roots (if you can get them), finely chopped

1 lime, juice

1 lime, cut in quarters to serve

5cm piece of ginger, peeled and minced

50g (1½oz/2 cups) fresh basil – Thai, Indian, lime, cinnamon, lemon if possible (otherwise use sweet basil)

2-3 tbsp sunflower or other light oil

Salt and pepper to taste

Add 140g (5oz/1 cup) of cashews or cooked pulses (lentils, dried peas, beans) to the curry along with vegetables if you wish.

Serve with rice or noodles.

Pour the oil into a large wok or saucepan. Add the onions, garlic, ginger and chillies. Stir and sauté until the onions are soft. Add the lemongrass, coriander roots and stems and stir.

Add the vegetables, coconut milk, stock, soy sauce, seasoning, bring to the boil then reduce the heat and simmer with a lid on for 30 minutes.

Meanwhile prepare the rice or noodles and any of the side dishes you wish.

When the curry is cooked, stir through the coriander leaves and the basil. Leave for five minutes and then serve.

WINTER VARIATION

Replace the summer vegetables with diced winter vegetables, you will need to add a little more water as winter vegetables tend to be less moist. Replace the basil with 1 cup of coriander leaves and 1 cup of parsley.

E.g. parsnip, squash, celeriac, potato, cauliflower, calabrese, turnip, swede, carrot.

Stuffed whole squash with roast potatoes, parsnips and red wine gravy

This takes rather a lot of preparation and makes an ideal celebration meal.

1 winter squash

240g (8½oz/1½ cups) cooked beans, or 225g (8oz/1½ cups) nuts, chopped or seeds

250g (8¾oz/2 cups) vegetables (diced carrots, swede, parsnip, kale, celeriac, etc.)

135g (4¾oz/1 cup) onions or leeks

2-4 cloves garlic, minced

100g (3½oz/½ cup) dried fruit (cranberries, raisins, dates, apricots)

2 tbsp herbs, freshly chopped (rosemary, thyme, sage, French tarragon, parsley, mint)

1 tbsp olive oil

Potatoes and parsnips, cut into chunks

2 tbsp oil

Seasonal vegetables

Food grade string for tying or cocktail sticks

RED WINE GRAVY

236ml (8¼fl.oz/1 cup) red wine

472ml (16½fl.oz/2 cups) vegetable stock

135g (4¾oz/1 cup) onions, sliced

1 stick celery, sliced

1 tbsp olive oil

2 cloves garlic

1 tbsp tamari or other soy sauce

1 tsp Dijon or other mustard

2 tbsp wholewheat flour (or gluten free flour)

A sprig each of thyme, rosemary, sage

2 bay leaves

2 tbsp redcurrant or cranberry jelly (optional)

Preheat the oven to 180°C fan (200°C/400°F/gas mark 6).

Pour the oil in a pan and sauté the onions and garlic until the onions are soft (about 10 minutes). Add the beans (or nuts or seeds), diced vegetables, herbs and fruit, chopping any larger pieces of dried fruit and stir. Remove from the heat.

Meanwhile, bring a pan of water to the boil and parboil the potatoes and parsnips for 10 minutes. Drain (reserve the liquid to cook the vegetables in) and shake the pan gently.

Cut the top off the squash, reserving to make a lid, and scoop out the seeds. Put in a large ovenproof dish.

Stuff with the filling, pressing down with a spoon to really fill the cavity. Replace the 'lid' and fasten with cocktail sticks or tie with string.

Place the potatoes and parsnips around the squash. Lightly coat with the oil, using a brush.

Put the tray in the oven for an hour, depending on the size of your squash. Check the potatoes and parsnips halfway through and turn over so that they become crispy all over.

Whilst it is cooking, prepare your gravy vegetables and make the gravy.

Pour the olive oil into the pan. Add the onion, carrot, garlic, celery and herbs. Sauté for about 10 minutes until the onions are soft, stirring to make sure the vegetables don't burn.

Add the flour and stir for one minute.

Remove from the heat and gradually incorporate the red wine, a tablespoon at a time, stirring thoroughly. There will be some lumps, so try to remove those with the stirring. A small hand whisk is useful here.

Add the stock, tamari and mustard. Bring to the boil and reduce the heat. Simmer for 10 minutes, whisking and stirring regularly to make a smooth gravy. Add the redcurrant jelly (if using)

Remove the herbs with a slotted spoon and pour into a gravy jug.

If you prefer a gravy without 'bits' in, pour through a sieve before serving.

If you prefer a gravy without wine, just replace with an extra cup of stock.

Stuffed gem squash

Gem squash grow prolifically, just one plant should be enough for a family. Early croppers, you start harvesting in the summer and they keep producing well into the autumn. The squash store well but are more difficult to get into as the skin hardens – we have eaten autumn harvested gem squash the following April.

Alternatively, stuff summer squash (patty pan, crookneck) or large courgettes. Any leftover stuffing is nice sprinkled on salads or over pasta or noodles.

4 gem squash

100g (3½oz/1 cup) leeks or onions, sliced

240g (8oz/1 cup) parsnip, potato, celeriac, or turnip, grated

240g (8oz/1 cup) carrot, grated

60ml (2fl.oz/¼ cup) olive oil

150g (5oz/1 cup) nuts, chopped or seeds (or 125g (4oz/1 cup) breadcrumbs)

2 tbsp parsley, finely chopped

2 cloves garlic (more if you wish)

Salt and pepper to taste

6-8 potatoes, washed and cut into chunky chips (optional)

Preheat the oven to 180°C fan (200°C/400°F/gas mark 6).

Cut the top off the squash and remove the seeds. Place in an ovenproof dish with the potatoes (if using). Drizzle the potatoes with a little oil to coat.

In a frying pan, heat the oil and add the onions and garlic. Sauté until the onion is soft, then add the grated vegetables. Stir for two minutes and remove from the heat. Stir through the breadcrumbs or nuts.

Spoon the mixture into the squash cavities and replace the tops.

Bake for 30 minutes until cooked.

Serve with salads or steamed vegetables.

These stuffed squashes are tasty cold too, so I usually bake extra for another meal.

Homegrown baked beans

These richly flavoured baked beans are delicious served on toast for breakfast, with chunky chips and salad or even with rice.

This recipe works well with all kinds of beans, including tinned (drain and rinse before cooking).

240g (8½oz/1½ cups) borlotti beans (cooked)

300g (10½oz/2 cups) chopped tomatoes (fresh, frozen or canned)

200g (7oz/1½ cups) onions, finely chopped

2 stalks celery, finely chopped

2-4 cloves garlic

236ml (8fl.oz/1 cup) water or stock – plus more if needed

60ml (2fl.oz/¼ cup) cider vinegar (or red wine vinegar)

60ml (2fl.oz/¼ cup) maple syrup

1 tbsp blackstrap molasses

1 tsp fresh rosemary leaves, finely chopped (or ½ tsp dried)

1 tsp thyme, finely chopped

1 tbsp wholegrain mustard

1 tsp smoked paprika

1 tsp ground cumin

1 tbsp olive oil

Salt and pepper to taste

Fresh parsley to serve

In a large pan, sauté the onions, celery and garlic until soft.

Add the rest of the ingredients and stir, bringing to the boil.

Reduce the heat, stir, replace the lid and cook on low for three hours. Check every 45 minutes or so to stir and make sure it is not drying out. If the baked beans do look too dry, add a little more water.

Sprinkle with chopped fresh parsley to serve.

TIP   In the winter if you have a woodburner that you can cook on, after bringing the baked beans to the boil move onto the woodburner to simmer.

If you are using canned beans, then simmer for one hour not three.

summer roast vegetable torte

Summer roast vegetable torte

A very flexible dish, tortes are made in a springform tin and so exact quantities of ingredients do not matter so much. Tortes look rather lovely and make excellent party and picnic dishes. Feel free to be as creative as you wish with the layering!

Bake this in a 20cm springform cake tin or a pie dish.

1 large aubergine, cut into 1.3cm rings

2 courgettes, cut into 0.7cm slices

2 summer squash, cut into 0.7cm slices

2 sweet peppers, cored, deseeded and cut into quarters

12 cherry tomatoes, cut in half

2 golden or Chioggia beetroot, cut into 1.3cm slices

2 red or white onions, peeled and cut into 0.7cm slices

2 cups spinach or chard, chopped

2-4 cloves garlic, thinly sliced

10 mushrooms, sliced

110ml (4fl.oz/½ cup) olive oil

25g (1oz/½ cup) basil leaves, chopped

Salt and pepper to taste

Preheat the oven to 180°C fan (200°C/400°F/gas mark 6).

Spread the vegetables (except the spinach) on baking sheets, brush with oil and roast on both sides until soft. Remove from the oven.

Brush the springform tin with oil. Starting with the aubergine, spread the vegetables in layers, sprinkling each layer with a little basil and garlic and seasoning.

Press the top to compact the torte and drizzle the top with olive oil.

Bake for 30 minutes and remove from the oven. Let the torte rest for five minutes, then remove the outer ring and leave for a further five minutes before cutting.

This is delicious hot and cold.

Winter vegetable torte

1 small swede, cut into 1.3cm slices

1 small squash, peeled if necessary, cut into 1.3cm slices

2 beetroot, cut into 1.3cm slices

1 parsnip, cut into 1.3cm slices

2 red or white onions, peeled and cut into 0.7cm slices

2 cups kale, chopped

2-4 cloves garlic, thinly sliced

10 mushrooms, sliced

110ml (4fl.oz/½ cup) olive oil

25g (1oz/½ cup) seasonal herbs, chopped

Salt and pepper to taste

Preheat the oven to 180°C fan (200°C/400°F/gas mark 6).

Spread the vegetables (except the kale) on baking sheets, brush with oil and roast on both sides until soft. Remove from the oven.

Brush the springform tin with oil. Starting with the swede, spread the vegetables in layers, sprinkling each layer with some herbs, garlic and seasoning.

Press the top to compact the torte and drizzle the top with olive oil.

Bake for 30 minutes and remove from the oven. Let the torte rest for five minutes, then remove the outer ring and leave for a further five minutes before cutting.

This is delicious hot and cold.

Roasted radicchio and sugar loaf chicory

This is one of my absolute favourites and is the main reason why I grow so many radicchios and chicories.

I always make a whole pan at a time to make several meals.

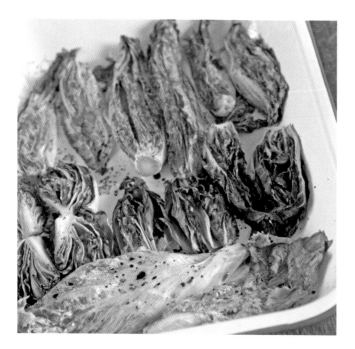

Firm, crisp radicchios and sugar loaf chicories, as many as will fit in your pan!

Olive oil

Salt and pepper to taste

Preheat the oven to 180°C fan (200°C/400°F/gas mark 6).

Cut the radicchios and chicories into quarters and arrange on an ovenproof dish

Drizzle with the olive oil. Add salt and pepper if you wish and roast for 15-20 minutes, until soft and starting to caramelise.

I like to eat these with crusty bread, just drizzled with olive oil. They are a delicious side for many of the recipes here.

Quick radicchio noodles

Half a roasted radicchio, chopped into chunks

Rice noodles

Tamari

Black pepper

Cook the noodles and drain. Add a few shakes of tamari and some black pepper and stir through the radicchio.

TIP For quick radicchio pasta, replace the tamari with balsamic vinegar.

Roasted radicchio risotto

The radicchio in this recipe can be replaced with roasted cabbage, if you wish.

300g (10½oz/1½ cups) Arborio rice

1 radicchio, cut into quarters and roasted

6 sun-dried tomatoes, chopped

135g (4¾oz/1 cup) red or white onions, finely chopped

2-4 cloves garlic, minced

1.2 litres (42fl.oz/5 cups) water or stock

140ml (8fl.oz/1 cup) white wine (or use stock)

1 tsp fresh thyme, finely chopped

1 tbsp olive oil

Salt and pepper to taste

Pour the oil into a large pan and sauté the onions and garlic with the thyme until the onion is soft. Add the rice and stir to coat with the oil.

Gradually pour in the wine and stock, ½ cup at a time, allowing the liquid to be absorbed by the rice before adding the next ½ cup.

After 15-20 minutes, add the radicchio and sun-dried tomatoes. Stir and cook for five minutes, adding a little more liquid if needed.

Taste and season.

Persian rhubarb stew 'Khoresh Rivas'

This stew is traditionally made with lamb so I have adapted it to include some of the vegetables that are available during rhubarb season. It is best to use fresh rhubarb as frozen will be too mushy, although that will make for an interesting sauce!

135g (4¾oz/1 cup) onions, chopped

400g (15oz) rhubarb, cut into 2.5cm pieces

140g (5oz/1 cup) potatoes, diced

280g (10oz/2 cups) turnip, diced
(or parsnip, swede, beetroot, carrot)

1 bunch chard (approx. 340g/12oz),
shredded (or spinach, cabbage leaves)

240g (8½oz/1½ cups) broad beans
(or other cooked beans)

2-4 cloves garlic, minced

50g (1½oz/1 cup) parsley, finely chopped

1 tbsp mint, finely chopped

½ tsp ground turmeric

1 tsp ginger, grated

700ml (25fl.oz/3 cups) stock

2 tbsp oil

Salt and pepper to taste

Heat the oil in a large pan and sauté the onions and garlic until soft. Add the turmeric, ginger and vegetables and cook for another two minutes, stirring.

Add the stock and bring to the boil. Reduce the heat and simmer for 15 minutes.

Next, add the parsley, mint and rhubarb. Stir and replace the lid. Cook for a further 15 minutes. Serve with a green salad and rice.

Sprouting stir fry

This simple meal is a regular quick lunch or supper dish in my house. I like it for breakfast too.

It's a great way of making the most of that spring purple sprouting broccoli glut as well as using sprouts from bolting brassicas (Brussel sprouts, kale), too.

500g (17½oz) purple sprouting broccoli or other sprouting greens

130g (4½oz/1 cup) cashew nuts or cooked beans or sliced mushrooms

135g (4¾oz/1 cup) onions, thinly sliced

180g (6oz/1 cup) carrots, grated

2-4 cloves garlic

2 tbsp sunflower oil

2 tbsp soy sauce

1cm peeled fresh ginger, minced

1-2 chilli, chopped (optional)

1 tbsp sesame oil (optional)

2 tbsp sesame or sunflower seeds

Freshly ground black pepper

1 lime, juice (optional)

Rice noodles (follow the directions on the packet) or rice

Cut the broccoli into florets and slice any thick stems.

Heat the sunflower oil in a wok or large frying pan. Add the onions, garlic, ginger and chilli and stir fry on a low heat until the onions are soft.

Add the nuts (or beans or mushrooms), carrot and soy sauce and stir fry for another 4-5 minutes.

Add the sesame oil, seeds and season with pepper (there is no need for salt as the soy sauce is salty). Pour on the lime juice if using and stir.

Serve over noodles or rice.

VARIATION

Replace the sprouting broccoli with cauliflower, chard, spinach or kale.

In the summer, add sliced sweet pepper.

Roast vegetable and lentil ragout

When I roast vegetables, I usually make the most of heating the oven by filling three trays and storing the surplus in the fridge or freezer. This is a great way of using vegetables that might be about to go past their best and means that there are plenty of cooked vegetables ready to make other dishes, saving time and energy. Roasting the vegetables adds an additional depth of sweetness and flavour to the dish.

This recipe is just as delicious using summer vegetables.

1kg (35oz/7 cups) root vegetables – parsnip, celeriac, kohl rabi, beetroot, carrot, diced

135g (4¾oz/1 cup) onion, sliced thinly

2-4 cloves garlic, minced

1 tsp chilli powder

¼ tsp cayenne powder (less if you want a less hot and spicy ragout)

½ tsp smoked paprika

210g (7½oz/1 cup) lentils – red, green or brown

1.2 litres (42fl.oz/5 cups) stock

4 tbsp olive oil

Salt and pepper to taste

2 tbsp fresh seasonal herbs to serve, finely chopped

Preheat the oven to 180°C fan (200°C/400°F/gas mark 6).

Dice the vegetables and spread on an ovenproof dish. Drizzle with 2 tbsp oil, making sure everything is lightly coated using your fingers or a brush.

Put in the oven for 15 minutes, then remove and add the sliced onions. Mix everything and return to the oven for a further 10 minutes. Remove from the oven.

Heat 2 tbsp oil in a large saucepan. Add the garlic and lentils and stir for a minute.

Add the roasted vegetables, spices and stock. Bring to the boil, reduce the heat and simmer for 25 minutes, stirring every now and then.

Season to taste, sprinkle over the fresh herbs and serve with mashed potatoes, rice or garlic bread.

TIP Add another cup of stock and blend using an immersion blender to make a nourishing soup.

If you prefer, fry the onion, garlic and celery in a large pan, add the diced raw vegetables and stir. Add the lentils, herbs, spices and stock and bring to the boil. Reduce the heat and simmer for 30-40 minutes, until the lentils and vegetables are cool.

VARIATION

Replace 500ml (2 cups) of stock with 500g (2 cups) of diced tomatoes in the summer.

Cider and vegetable casserole

I live in Somerset, famous for its historical apple cider orchards. The cider adds richness and flavour to this delicious winter casserole. Serve with mashed potato, couscous or crusty bread.

For a summer version, replace the parsnips, leeks and celeriac with turnips, new potatoes and courgette.

500ml apple cider

Cooked chickpeas, carlin peas or beans

135g (4¾oz/1 cup) onions, chopped

240g (8½oz/2½ cups) leeks, chopped

2 sticks celery, sliced

2-4 cloves garlic, minced

500g (17½oz/4 cups) root vegetables, cubed – carrot, parsnip, celeriac, swede, turnip

2 apples, cored and sliced

2 tbsp oil (olive, sunflower)

1 tbsp fresh sage, chopped

1 tsp thyme leaves, chopped

1 bay leaf

Salt and pepper to taste

Heat the oil in a large casserole pan and sauté the onions, leeks, celery and garlic until soft.

Add the rest of the vegetables and herbs; stir then add the chickpeas (peas or beans) and pour in the cider. Season, bring to the boil then reduce the heat to a simmer.

Cook over a low heat for 45 minutes.

Alternatively, cook in the oven at 180°C fan (200°C/400°F/gas mark 6) for 1½ hours.

5

DRINKS

Whether you are growing some of your own food, foraging in the hedgerows or exploring local markets for seasonal ingredients, making your own drinks adds another delicious dimension to the kitchen. Here I share some recipes to inspire you to make your own tea blends, infused waters and alcoholic beverages.

cucumber,
mint and
borage
infused water

INFUSED WATER

Infused waters make refreshing thirst-quenching drinks, look beautiful and taste fantastic. They are so simple to make and easy to adapt to your own and your family's preferences.

Just like plants, we need water in order to thrive and function properly. Plain water is refreshing and keeps us hydrated. Infused waters add something extra: not only great flavours but also added vitamins, minerals and other properties, depending what ingredients you choose.

Infused waters may also encourage people who think that plain water is 'boring' to drink more. They can be cheap to make – I often use the ends of fruit that I am using for other things to make an infused water, making the most of my produce.

All of these recipes are sugar free and use natural ingredients. They are (almost!) all homegrown too.

Infused waters keep in the fridge for a week. You can top up the water as needed. Gradually the flavours will reduce; then pour the fruit and herbs into the compost bin, clean the jar and try a different combination.

Use filtered water if you can. Our water is safe to drink but does contain chlorine and other chemicals that can affect the flavour. I have a Berkey water filter in my kitchen – the filters last for 10 years – it is almost plastic free and worked out cheaper in the long run than the plastic jug water filter I was using before. (I also live in a hard water area so filtering the water reduces limescale and prolongs the life of my kettle.)

If you do not have a filter, fill a jug with water and leave for 24 hours. Boiling the water first speeds up this process. This helps the chlorine to evaporate and improves the flavour.

If I am somewhere where I cannot filter the water or let it evaporate, such as a B&B, I just fill up my jug regardless and don't worry.

TIPS Do try to use organic ingredients as much as possible to keep your infusions pesticide free. If you are not sure about the provenance of your fruit, herbs or vegetables, give them a good wash (see pages 4-5) and peel where possible.

You can use frozen fruit, especially on a hot day.

You will need:

A container:
>glass jugs or pitchers; mason jars; large jam jars.

A muddler or similar for mashing.

A lid is useful especially if the jars are left at room temperature but you can always pop something on the top of a lidless jug (a jam jar lid, saucer, napkin).

When out and about you could use:

Glass water infuser bottle – ideal for taking to work, the gym, when going out and about, – these come with a metal skewer to fix the ingredients in place, or an infuser core, both of which stop the ingredients from blocking up the bottle top that you drink out of.

BPA free infuser bottle or cup – plastic, but some places do not allow glass bottles, such as pop concerts, schools, some gyms.

Metal infuser bottle.

Ingredients

FRUIT AND VEGETABLES

Florence fennel - lemon - lime - orange - grapefruit - tangerine - cucumber - pear - apple - plum - carrot - celery - blueberries - apricots - blackberries - blackcurrants - redcurrants - greengages - tomatoes - melon - cherries - strawberries - nectarines - mango - pineapple …

BOTANICALS, HERBS AND SPICES

Basil - lemongrass - lemon verbena - lemon balm - black pepper - rosemary - thyme - vanilla beans - ginger - mint - lavender - cinnamon - cardamom - chilli - sage - coriander - chamomile - calendula - sweet cicely - stevia - fennel - rose - parsley - cloves - viola …

Some infusion combinations

There are no exact recipes as the quantities depend on the size of your container and personal preference. As a guide, gently crush (just a little, to release the flavour!) your chopped ingredients, fill up to ¼ of your container with fruit, veg and herbs and top up with water.

rose petal and cardamom infused water

Tomato, cucumber and basil (or mint)
Orange and vanilla bean
Lemon and ginger
Lime and mint
Pear, vanilla and ginger
Lavender, lemon and rose petal
Viola, strawberry and lemon verbena
Apple and cinnamon
Blackberry, apple and ginger
Orange, black pepper and ginger
Pineapple and mint
Blackcurrant and rosemary
Rose petal and cardamom
Orange, lemon and lime

Tomato, celery, black pepper and chilli
Lemon and thyme
Cucumber, ginger and mint
Orange and rosemary

JUST HERBS

Mint and lemon balm
Lemongrass, ginger and mint
Rosemary, thyme and parsley
Thai basil, holy basil and lime basil
Sage, mint and thyme
Lemon verbena, lemon balm and lemon basil
Parsley, mint and fennel

HOMEMADE, HOMEGROWN AND FORAGED HERBAL TEA BLENDS

Herbal teas have been enjoyed for centuries to refresh, revive and also medicinally, to treat physical, mental and emotional health. I am not a trained medical herbalist and so here I am suggesting tea blends that taste delicious, but will mention some of the traditional uses of some of the herbs for information. Although all of these ingredients are natural, if you are pregnant, breastfeeding or on medication, do check with a qualified medical practitioner to be advised if there are any herbs that you need to avoid. None of these teas are designed to replace qualified medical treatment or diagnosis.

Today, we are becoming increasingly aware of the plastics used in many herbal tea bags. The first I knew of this was finding 'ghost tea bags' in my compost heaps when spreading the mulch on my beds! These need removing and sadly putting in the rubbish for landfill. Making your own herb teas reduces single use plastics.

Homemade herbal teas taste quite unlike anything that you buy in the shops, especially when using freshly picked herbs and flowers. The taste is vibrant and exciting and you can be sure that good quality ingredients have been used.

Dried, they are easy to store in recycled glass jars. I usually store everything separately and then make up my own blends, but you can also store as ready mixed blends. These make lovely, thoughtful gifts too.

Fortunately, most of the herbs and flowers mentioned here are not hard to grow or forage for (or buy from shops or online) and all are easy to dry to prolong the season and provide you with refreshing beverages throughout the winter months.

Equipment

You will probably have most of the equipment needed to make herbal teas.

- **Teapot** – it's best to have a separate one for herbs and regular tea, if you can. I like to use glass teapots with a glass infuser: this is known as a tisaniere, you can see the herbs as they are infusing and decide when the tea is ready. An ordinary teapot is absolutely fine but you will need a …

- **Tea strainer** or an **infusing ball** – these come in different sizes and are usually made from stainless steel. Larger ones are ideal for teapots (I also use one for my herbal bath teas, see page 192) and smaller for individual cups. Get one with plenty of holes: some of the fun shaped infusers do not have many holes and don't work very well as an infuser.

- **Infusing cup** – these are cups with a separate china infuser and a lid, designed for making single cups of tea.

- **Measuring spoons** – I use the ones I already have for cooking.

- **Pestle and mortar** – I use both large and small heavy stone pestle and mortars.

- **Spice/coffee grinder** – one that is just used for herbs if possible as the coffee taste will come through. I use an attachment that comes with my immersion blender.

- **Kettle**

- **Measuring jug**

- **Glass storage jars and labels**

- **A dehydrator** – this is very useful, but you can also easily air dry the herbs.

Tea Ingredient Suggestions

Mint (*Mentha*)

A fast growing perennial herb, there are so many different kinds of mints – chocolate mint, apple mint, peppermint, gingermint, to name a few. I grow lots of different varieties in pots around my garden. They are highly invasive and will take over if planted in the ground. They will grow happily in pots on a windowsill indoors.

Mint is refreshing and good for the digestion. It is a great tea for starting the day or after a meal.

Fennel (*Foeniculum vulgare*)

Fennel is a very tall perennial herb that looks stunning in a flower border. During the winter it dies back, leaving many hollow, dried stalks. These are perfect habitat for many overwintering insects including ladybirds. It's too tall to grow indoors, but dries well.

Use the leaves, flowers and seeds in teas. Fennel is an excellent digestive.

Lemon balm (*Melissa officinalis*)

A delicious lemon scented perennial herb, lemon balm can have green or golden variegated leaves. It is invasive and so it's best grown in pots. Use the leaves in teas. Grow indoors or outside.

Lemon balm is calming and a digestive. A cup of tea daily is said to improve the memory! It can be helpful for menstrual cramps and for those prone to cold sores.

Lemongrass (*Cymbopogon*)

One of my favourite tea herbs, this tropical plant is possible to grow from seed but requires heat, so if you don't have a greenhouse then plants are widely available. I grow lemongrass in my polytunnel and in pots. In the UK it is mainly an annual herb, dying in the winter. It likes sun!

Lemongrass tea is good for the digestion, making it an excellent after dinner brew. It is often used as a healthy tea to help with the symptoms of colds, containing vitamin C and antibacterial properties.

Rosemary (*Rosemarinus officinalis*)

An aromatic, woody, evergreen perennial herb, rosemary can be grown and harvested outside year round. It flowers early in the spring, providing helpful food for bees and other insects. I often find that ladybirds choose to hibernate in rosemary bushes too; come out to 'sunbathe' on sunny days.

Rosemary tea can be helpful for the brain and is especially useful for activities that require memory and mental exertion. Inhaling the tea helps to clear the head during periods of intense concentration. It is a digestive, especially useful if you have excess gas. The tea makes a good skin wash too, especially for dry, flaky skin.

Rose (*Rosa*)

Any aromatic garden rose can be used to make teas. Rose petals and hips are both used fresh and dried. Do make sure that you use only unsprayed flowers and check for insects before making a brew, shaking the flowers carefully to dislodge them – aphids floating in a cup of tea is not very appealing!

Rose petal tea has vitamins C, A and E and is good for the skin (you can use it as a face splash too). It's helpful if you have a cold or sore throat and can also help with digestion and menstrual cramps. It's calming and refreshing, good to have after a stressful day.

Lavender (*Lavendula*)

Lavender is a highly perfumed woody perennial herb. Its purple flowers attract beneficial insects and, traditionally, laundry was dried on large lavender bushes to infuse the clothes with its

mint

lemongrass

rosemary

lavender

scented pelargonium

gem marigold

calendula

lemon verbena

basil

fragrance. The leaves and especially flowers are used to make tea and a range of other edible dishes (put a few sprigs in a jam jar of sugar, replace the lid and leave for two weeks, shaking every day, to make a divine smelling lavender sugar).

Lavender tea is soothing and helpful for anxiety and stress. It can help to induce sleep and relaxation and is also good for the digestion. The tea is also beneficial cooled and used as a hair rinse, to promote hair growth and a healthy scalp.

Scented geranium/pelargonium
(*Pelargonium* 'Graveolens', 'Attar of Roses', 'Sweet Mimosa', Crispum and many others)

Pelargoniums are half hardy perennials. I grow mine in pots so that they can easily be brought into the house for the winter as they are killed by cold weather. Indoors, the pelargoniums die back, so remove leaves and flowers to dry for winter use and prune. Keep the pots in a warm place until the spring, when they will start to shoot again. When all danger of frost has passed, the pelargonium pots can be moved outside where they will enjoy a sunny location. The leaves and flowers are used fresh or dried to make teas and a range of herbal infusions and potions, including the Tussie Mussie on page 191.

The taste and scent of the pelargoniums vary according to the variety. Rose scented geraniums are very popular for teas and culinary use; other scents and flavours include almond, lemon, strawberry, mint, pineapple and hazelnut.

Not all pelargoniums and geraniums are safe to eat. Be sure to buy a recognised named variety from a reputable source.

Scented pelargonium tea is calming and can help reduce feelings of anxiety or being overwhelmed. It can be helpful for sore throats. The fresh leaves, slightly bruised and rubbed on the skin help to soothe insect bites.

Gem marigolds
(*Tagetes tenufolia* 'Lemon Gem', 'Starfire')

'Lemon Gem' and 'Starfire' are my favourite edible marigolds. Also known as 'signet marigolds', the small plants are full of flavour: in my work kitchen garden they are popular with the chefs and bar staff. These annuals are easy to grow from seed. I sow in early May to plant out when the danger of frost has passed (mid-May here in Somerset, you need to check for your local frost dates). The seeds are easy to save in the autumn for sowing the following spring. Grow gem marigolds under cover and outside: they attract beneficial insects into the garden and can help deter some pests, including white fly. Use the flowers to make teas.

The flowers are used for their flavour and colour.

Pot marigold/calendula
(*Calendula officinalis*)

Calendula is a highly beneficial annual herb. It will overwinter in a polytunnel or greenhouse, but is killed by frost in the garden. However, the seeds survive in the soil and will sprout the following spring; it is easy to hoe off, if it is becoming too invasive. The flowers come in a variety of shades of orange, yellow and red: all are edible and can be used widely in the kitchen and to make infused oils, salves and other healthful solutions. Dry the petals to use during the winter. The taste is a little earthy and unusual, so it can benefit from being mixed with another stronger tasting herb to brighten the flavour.

Calendula tea is beneficial for the skin and can help to boost your immune system. It has some anti-inflammatory properties and can help to settle stomach ache. The tea is calming and can soothe an anxious mood. Cooled tea makes a refreshing skin splash.

Lemon verbena (*Aloysia citrodora*)

A perennial plant from South America, lemon verbena can be killed by a harsh winter and so I grow mine in pots and bring into the house, greenhouse or polytunnel during the winter. Prune and dry the fragrant leaves. The plant will then look quite dead until April or May, when new growth can be observed. Lemon verbena has a powerful lemony scent, so vibrant it tastes rather like a lemon flavoured sherbet.

It almost fizzes in the mouth! The tea is divine; fresh and lively.

Lemon verbena tea can help to reduce inflammation in the joints, aid digestion and help reduce uncomfortable symptoms from cramping, bloating and flatulence. It is calming, soothing and helps to reduce stress. The tea is considered to be beneficial to drink before and after exercise.

Basil (Ocimum basilicum)

There are an extraordinary number of basil varieties to choose from, too many to list here and all have their own flavour. Lemon, lime, Thai, liquorice, sweet and Holy basil are some especially tasty varieties. Basil is an annual, dying as the days cool and shorten, although it can be grown indoors over winter with warmth and light. It is easy to dry too for winter use. You can use the leaves, stems and flowers in teas.

The tea is good for oral health, including helping to promote fresh breath. It helps to improve the health of skin and relaxes and soothes. It is a good bedtime tea and can help make you feel a little better if you have winter colds and bugs.

Blue butterfly pea (Clitorea ternatea)

An annual tropical flower, blue butterfly pea can be rather tricky to grow as it loves warmth and sunlight. I grow it in my polytunnel, sowing the seeds in late April on heat. It requires support from pea sticks just like garden peas. The lapis lazuli blue flowers are a delight to behold and produce the most incredible natural blue tea and food colouring. I came across this beautiful edible flower in Thailand, where it is widely used as a healing tea and natural blue dye for cakes, rice and other dishes. The dried flowers are widely available if you do not have the space undercover to grow your own.

The tea has the extraordinary property of turning a vibrant ultra violet with the addition of a little lemon or lime juice.

The tea has antioxidants, rather like green tea, which are considered to be good for overall health. It is considered to be stimulating and energising, good for the brain. It is beneficial

for the skin, helps to reduce the symptoms of headaches and inflammation and reduces stress and anxiety. Blue butterfly pea tea is said to be an aphrodisiac!

Thyme
(Thymus vulgaris and many other varieties)

This aromatic, perennial evergreen has many traditional medical uses as well as culinary and ornamental. It is easy to grow from seed or buy small plants that establish themselves quickly. You can pick thyme year round outside. Choose different varieties which each have their own flavour, including lemon, orange and caraway. The flowers are tiny, very pretty and attractive to bees and other beneficial insects.

Thyme tea has been used medically for thousands of years. It has a strong flavour that can take some getting used to. I drink it whenever I have a sore throat (it's a good gargle for this too) and have come to love it, but do add a teaspoon of something sweet to improve the flavour, should you wish. It can help to soothe colds, boost the immune system and digestion and reduce stomach ache. The tea is said to be good for the brain and memory.

Stevia (Stevia rebaudiana)

Stevia is an extremely sweet leafy perennial herb; a member of the Asteraceae family which includes dandelions, sunflowers and lettuce. Grown from seed sown on heat in early spring, it takes a long time to germinate so be patient. Keep the seedlings and young plants frost free. Stevia grows best in pots undercover on a windowsill or in the greenhouse or polytunnel. Alternatively, you can propagate from cuttings. In the late autumn the plant will die back; prune hard and keep in a frost free place (I keep mine on a windowsill in the house) and it will start to shoot again in early spring. The leaf tastes very sweet with an aniseed or liquorice accent.

The leaves are used fresh or dried along with other herbs to naturally sweeten teas and other beverages. Use one or two bruised fresh leaves or a tiny pinch of dried.

blue butterfly pea

thyme

stev

shiso

red perilla

nett

meadowsweet

elder

red clove

Sweet cicely (*Myrrhis odorata*)

Sweet cicely is an aromatic, perennial herb that dies back in winter and emerges to flower in early spring, around the same time as early rhubarb. The early flowers are much appreciated by bees and other insects. The herb is traditionally used to sweeten rhubarb, reducing or eliminating sugar in recipes. All parts of the plant are used including the roots (roasted like parsnip) with the leaves, flowers and torpedo shaped young green seed pods, to sweeten food and drinks. I like to chew on the aniseed flavoured seed pods; refreshing on a hot day. Sweet cicely is invasive but easy to weed out if it appears in unwanted locations.

The tea made with leaves, flowers or green pods is traditionally used to cheer and lift the spirits. It can soothe and calm stomach pain, aid digestion and reduce flatulence.

Shiso also known as Perilla (*Perilla frutescens*)

A member of the mint family (Lamiaceae), shiso is widely used in Japanese and Korean cuisine. Shiso is an annual herb in the UK. Sow on gentle heat in the spring at the same time as basil and grow under cover until the danger of frost has passed. Shiso will grow reasonably well outside, reaching great heights if grown in a polytunnel (last year it was almost as tall as me!). The jagged leaves resemble stinging nettles. Green shiso has a stronger flavour than its red/purple cousin, rather like a citrus-coriander with a dash of cinnamon. The red shiso is slightly more bitter.

Red perilla makes a purple (or pink if mixed with lemon or lime juice) tea; green perilla is a pale green. It is traditionally used to relieve headaches, coughs, stuffy noses, colds and stomach upsets.

Gathering ingredients from the wild

As with all foraging, do make sure that you have properly identified any herb, flower, leaf or fruit before harvesting. Many poisonous wild plants grow alongside edible ones. Always try to pick wild plants away from areas of pollution, such as busy roads.

Stinging nettle (*Urtica dioica*)

Nettles are herbaceous, perennial plants, dying back in the winter and emerging in late winter/early spring. They can grow up to 2 metres tall and are widespread in rural and urban locations. Nettles provide food for the larvae of many butterflies and moths including the small tortoiseshell and peacock. Stinging nettles make an excellent plant tonic and are a useful addition to the compost heap.

Nettle is a diuretic. The tea can be useful for relieving the symptoms of hay fever and it is a general tonic for colds and feeling under the weather. It can help the skin and hair.

Meadowsweet (*Filipendula ulmaria*)

Meadowsweet is a perennial herb which grows widely in the countryside, especially on verges and along the banks of ditches and streams. It is a member of the Rosaceae family and is said to have been revered by the Druids. It was used to flavour mead; its folk name is 'mead wort' and is one of the strewing herbs, used to cover earth floors, for its insect repelling properties. Meadowsweet flowers in late spring, the rich creamy-white flowers giving off a gorgeous honey-almond scent.

Meadowsweet tea is made with the leaves and flowers. It is a digestive and can help to boost the immune system. It helps to relieve the symptoms of colds and is an anti-inflammatory.

Elder (*Sambucus nigra*)

Elder is a widespread tree with strongly scented leaves that are rather unpleasant. The tree flowers in late May and early June, abundant frothy blossoms which are often used to make a country sparkling wine and cordial, and they also make a healing salve infused in oil. Later in the year, in early autumn, the tree is filled with deep-purple berries which make a fantastic wine and herbal tonic. Dried berries can be used in place of raisins and other dried fruits in many recipes.

Elderflower tea helps to reduce the symptoms of hayfever and is a good tonic for the skin and blood. this refreshing brew also makes a helpful skin splash when cool. Soak a cloth in cooled elderflower tea and place on closed eyes to help soothe soreness and itchiness.

Elderberries are rich with vitamins; an abundant source of vitamin C. The tea is good for colds and is a good tonic for winter chills.

Dandelion (Taraxacum officinalis)

Dandelions are a widespread flowering perennial; a member of the Asteraceae family. They flower in early spring, providing an essential source of food for bees and other insects. Although I do not let them grow in my vegetable beds, I am happy to have dandelions growing in the wild edges of my garden for the bees and also to make tea, wine and cosmetics. So most of my dandelion 'foraging' is actually done at home or in Charles' garden, the lawns are bright with flowering weeds and buzzing with bees: dandelions, clover, daisies and buttercups. Finches and other small birds love to eat the dandelion seeds. I make tea from the petals. The roots can be used to make a coffee substitute.

Dandelion tea is a diuretic. It can help to improve digestion, reduce inflammation and give the immune system a boost.

Red clover (Trifolium pratense)

Red clover is a widespread herbaceous perennial flowering plant. It is an important pollinator for bees and other insects. It is used as a green manure and as a fodder crop. The flowerheads are used to make tea.

Red clover tea is considered to be helpful for women during menopause. It can help relieve congestion and coughing. It is calming and can help promote healthy skin.

Wild rose (Rosa canina)

Also known as 'dog roses', the wild rose is the name generally given to a variety of members of the rose family which grow wild. It is a fast growing perennial. Wild roses have five petals, usually pink, and very sharp thorns so do take care. As with cultivated roses, teas are made from the petals and rose hips. The petals can be used to make infused oils and creams for the body.

Rose hip tea is full of vitamin C and makes a great winter tonic to help reduce the symptoms of colds and coughs.

Silver Birch (Betula pendula)

The silver birch is a native deciduous tree with thin branches and a pale white, papery bark. When my children were young, we learned on bushcraft courses to use the dried bark as fire-lighting material. The buds, leaves and twigs are used to make tea.

Silver birch tea is a diuretic, anti-inflammatory and can help to ease joint pain. It helps digestion and boosts immunity. Silver birch contains vitamin C and beneficial minerals. The tea cleanses the blood and can help promote a restful sleep.

Pine (Pinus)

Pines are evergreen trees with fragrant dark green needles. The crushed needles can be used to make a fragrant infused oil and vinegar: they are excellent as an ingredient in homemade household cleansing sprays. Simmer a pan of needles in water on the stove to clear the air, especially useful in winter if the house is feeling stuffy.

The young needles, crushed and chopped, make a refreshing tea full of vitamin C and A. It is good for colds, clears the head (good to boost concentration when working) and helps to soothe coughs and colds.

Blackberry (*Rubus*)

Blackberries, also known as brambles, are a widespread perennial fruit growing in abandoned lots, hedgerows and other wild areas. Usually covered with sharp prickles, there are domesticated, spineless varieties which are more suitable for home growing. The fruit starts ripening from mid-summer right through the autumn. Pick the jewel coloured fruit when they are a dark purple. You can use the young leaves and ripe fruit to make tea.

Blackberry leaf tea helps to ease stomach pains and reduce flatulence. It soothes a sore throat and inflammation of the gums. The tea is said to help improve the memory and boost the immune system.

Blackberry fruit tea is rich with vitamins including A, C and E. The tea helps to relieve the symptoms of colds and coughs and is a delicious autumn and winter tonic.

Chickweed (*Stellaria media*)

Chickweed is a small, annual flowering weed with tiny leaves and white flowers, a relation of the carnation (family Caryophyllaceae). It produces a lot of seeds which spread extensively, making this a widespread and familiar plant. Although it can grow year round, it is mainly growing from spring until the early winter. It seems to grow everywhere and you are very likely to have plenty in your garden or allotment! It is delicious and full of vitamins; a valuable addition to salads and has many herbal uses. Use the leaves and flowers to make the tea.

Chickweed tea is soothing and detoxifying. It has high nutritional value, being rich in vitamins and minerals. It is a good tonic to help relieve and soothe symptoms of colds, hay fever and itchy skin conditions.

Additions from the kitchen, including:

Citrus – Peppercorns – Ginger root – Vanilla pods – Maple syrup and other sweeteners

Some tea blends

These blends are all for fresh leaves or flowers (unless otherwise stated); halve the quantity if using dried. The quantities make enough for one teapot.

Thyme, ginger and stevia

1 tbsp thyme leaves

2cm piece of ginger root, sliced

1-2 stevia leaves (or a pinch of dried stevia)

Lavender and mint

1 tbsp lavender flowers and leaves

1 tbsp mint

Very lemon tea

1 tbsp lemon balm leaves

1 tbsp lemon verbena leaves

1 sprig lemon thyme

Sleepytime tea

2 tbsp rose petals

1 tbsp chamomile flowers

After dinner tea

1 tbsp fennel seeds

1 tbsp mint leaves

2cm piece of ginger root, sliced

Red shiso tea

2 tbsp fresh shiso leaves

1 tbsp lemon juice

Sweet cicely and fennel

1 tbsp sweet cicely

1 tbsp fennel leaves

Blue butterfly pea tea

1 tbsp blue butterfly pea flowers (dried)

1 slice lemon or lime

Mojito tea

1 tbsp chocolate mint

1 tbsp lime basil

2 slices of lime

Floral tea

1 tsp lavender

1 tbsp rose petals

1 tsp gem marigolds

1 tsp calendula

making
elderberry
liqueur

HOMEMADE INFUSED ALCOHOL

Infusing homegrown fruits, herbs, spices, flowers and other ingredients in alcohol is a simple way of preserving the harvest, they last a very long time and make interesting gifts. Flavoured spirits and liqueurs are very popular, yet many do not realise how simple they are to make. They also look lovely, often bright jewel colours with delicious aromas.

Always use a good quality spirit: gin, vodka, rum, whisky or brandy. A poor quality alcohol could make you feel ill, and there are many reasonably priced 'own brand' spirits which have a good reputation. Organic spirits are widely available or buy from a small artisan maker. Vodka is the most neutral flavoured of the spirits; the others will all lend something of their own flavour to your concoction.

You will need:
- Large jars with lids
- A sieve or colander lined with muslin for filtering
- Your alcohol
- The ingredients
- Sugar
- Funnels for pouring into the jars and bottles
- Clean labelled bottles for storing – I use empty spirits bottles from local bars, cleaned.

TIP Do not discard the infused fruit! This can be used in baking and desserts.

I always use an unbleached organic sugar to make my infused liqueurs. This does colour the lighter infusions such as rose or rhubarb a little, but I am happy with that.

Prepare your ingredients

Fruit – wash, check for any signs of decay and remove lurking insects. Remove berries from the stems and gently crush them when they are inside the infusing jar. Cut larger fruit into chunks, removing the stones if applicable. Slice citrus fruit.

Herbs – gently shake to remove any insects. Rinse and allow to dry for a while on clean cloths. Bruise a little with a muddler or similar before adding to the brew.

Flowers – harvest when fully open before the sun is too strong, if you can. Shake gently to remove insects.

Infusion times

These vary depending on the ingredients. Usually I infuse a fruit based liqueur for two to three months.

Use the produce of your garden, the hedgerows, windowsill herb gardens or seasonal bargains from markets and shops to inspire your own infusion blends. Here are some of my favourites.

Spiced elderberry whisky liqueur

A deep-red, warmly spiced drink that tastes delicious drunk neat in tiny glasses (it is strong!) or as a nurturing hot toddy if you are feeling under the weather during the winter months. It makes a great cocktail too; try mixing with ginger beer.

Rich with vitamins, elderberries have been used for centuries to make healing brews for winter colds and chills. I like to think the healing properties are in this spicy cordial, especially as it also includes herbs and fruit well known for their medicinal benefits. I use it as a 'cure' for colds, flu and wintry bugs. I can't say for certain that a glass of this beside the fire on a dark January day does count as one of your 'five a day', but it certainly feels good.

I have been making versions of this delicious brew for about 12 years now. All I remember is that it is based on a recipe from Michigan. My children were smaller then and life is so busy with young children, time flies. You think "Oh, I'll make a note of that" and then suddenly it is 12 years later on and they are all grown up! And so I don't quite recall how I first came across mixing whisky with elderberries and spices.

If made when the elderberries are first ripe, this will be ready by mid-December, ideal for festive gifts.

YOU WILL NEED

1 litre (35¼fl.oz) of whisky or bourbon (or brandy, gin, vodka if you prefer)

1 litre (35¼fl.oz) of elderberries

1 organic orange, peel (so you know there are no chemicals or waxes on it)

1 organic lemon, peel

A piece of fresh ginger root, about the length of your thumb

6 cardamom pods

12 cloves

1 long stick of cinnamon (or 2 shorter ones)

100g (3½oz) unbleached sugar

A very large glass jar with a lid, thoroughly cleaned

The quantities need not be exact; if you have just over or under a litre of fruit that's fine too. To vary the flavours, reduce the elderberries and add blackberries or ripe rose hips (top and tail the rose hips before adding to the brew). All of these fruit are full of vitamins and autumnal gorgeousness.

Roughly chop the peel and ginger.

Crush the cardamom pods gently with a pestle or rolling pin.

A wide mouthed preserving funnel is great for making sure that all of the ingredients end up in the jar and not all over the table and floor. It is amazing how far squashed elderberry can travel when attached to socks!

Pour the ingredients into the jar in alternating layers.

Pour in the whisky, stir and admire.

Replace the lid. Put your beautiful brew away from direct sunlight but somewhere you'll see it fairly regularly so you can shake it every now and then. I store my brews on the dresser in the living room.

Leave for 3-4 months, strain through a sieve or muslin lined colander and store in labelled glass bottles. It will last for a very long time, but is usually gone by the following elderberry season.

TIP This works perfectly well with defrosted home frozen elderberries.

Replace the sweet cicely with 8 tbsp rose petals for a rhubarb and rose gin.

You can use vodka instead, if you prefer.

Rhubarb and sweet cicely gin

1 litre (35fl.oz) of gin

300g (10½oz) sugar

1kg (35oz) rhubarb

4 tbsp sweet cicely flowers, pods, leaves and stems (optional)

A very large glass lidded jar, thoroughly cleaned

Wash the rhubarb then slice into 3cm pieces.

Place in the large jar. Sprinkle over the sweet cicely and sugar.

Pour over the gin and stir.

Replace the lid and leave somewhere out of direct sunlight for 2-4 weeks (depending how strong you like the flavour).

Strain through a muslin lined colander and pour into labelled bottles.

Drink with your favourite tonic water or sparkling water. It feels like summer in a glass.

Sugar plum brandy

500g (17½oz) ripe plums

300g (10½oz) sugar

1 litre (35fl.oz) brandy

2 sticks cinnamon

A very large glass lidded jar, thoroughly cleaned

Wash the plums and pierce with a skewer all over.

Place in the jar with the sugar and cinnamon. Pour over the brandy and stir.

Replace the lid and leave somewhere out of direct sunlight for two months.

Strain through a muslin lined colander and pour into labelled bottles.

TIP   This makes a lovely after dinner liqueur as well as a cocktail base. For an especially decadent fruit cake, soak the fruit in this brandy for 24 hours before baking. I also use it to 'feed' my fruit cakes after baking.

Lemongrass, kaffir lime and basil rum

This is influenced by a delicious cocktail I drank sitting at a table on the pavement outside the Three Nagas Restaurant in Luang Prabang, Laos watching the vibrant street life, waiting for my dinner (which was fabulous too).

1 litre (35fl.oz) white rum

3 fresh lemongrass stalks, bashed with a rolling pin to crush

3 tbsp basil – preferably Thai, lemon or lime

6 kaffir lime leaves (or the peel of one lime)

200g (7oz) sugar

A very large glass lidded jar, thoroughly cleaned

TIP I grow kaffir lime in pots in the polytunnel during the summer, bringing it in for the winter. It will be happy outside too during summer months but is killed by hard frost.

Place all of the ingredients in the jar and stir.

Replace the lid and leave for two to three weeks, somewhere out of direct sunlight. The longer you leave it, the stronger the infusion.

Strain through a muslin lined colander and pour into labelled bottles.

This is delicious with tonic water or ginger ale, or use it as a base to make this cocktail, based on the spicy signature cocktail I enjoyed in Laos.

Lemongrass and kaffir lime leaves are easy to grow and also widely available in shops.

Creative kitchen cocktail

60ml (2fl.oz) lemongrass, kaffir lime and basil rum

30ml (1fl.oz) vodka

1-3 thin slices of chilli (optional)

1 kaffir lime leaf or 3 basil leaves

1 tbsp lime juice

1 slice lime to garnish

1 stick lemongrass, slightly crushed or split with a knife (see photo) to make a stirrer

1 tbsp lychee syrup or elderflower cordial

TIP Make a lemongrass straw to sip the cocktail. Carefully remove the outer layer of the lemongrass and roll into a tube.

OK, I know that it is unlikely that most of us will have lychee syrup on hand! You could use 1 tinned lychee and a little of the syrup that they came in. In my homegrown version, replace with 1 tbsp of elderflower or rose petal cordial.

Mix together the cordial (or syrup), rum, vodka and lime juice using the lemongrass. Pour into a chilled glass with the lime slice, chilli and lemongrass. Add ice.

Three Nagas cocktail, Laos

Herb and flower infused vodka

I like to make these herb infused vodkas in smaller jars so that I can experiment with more herbs (otherwise it can get too expensive!)

Choose from any of the herbs and flowers you grow. Mix to create your own combinations (look at the infused water and herb tea recipes for some combination ideas). My especial favourites are:

Lemon balm
Lemon verbena
Basil – all of the flavours
Mint – all of the flavours
Thyme – all of the flavours
Rosemary
Lavender
Dill
Sweet cicely
French tarragon
Rosemary
Elderflower
Rose petals
Coriander (leaves, green seeds and flowers)
Cumin (leaves, green seeds and flowers)

Vodka

An assortment of clean jars with lids

Labels

Herbs (see above)

Place 4-5 sprigs of your herbs (about 2cm shorter than the length of the jar) or 1 cup of petals/flowers in the jar. Top up with vodka until submerged. Place somewhere you'll remember to shake them daily, such as close to the kettle. Shake gently every day for 2-3 weeks and strain as recommended.

TIP Place something on top of the herbs to keep them submerged. A smaller glass lid could be perfect, or a smooth, flat, washed stone.

rose,
lemon,
verbena
and
mint
infused
vodka

Rose and
Lemon Verbena
Infused Vodka

Dried herb, flower and fruit infused spirits kit

This is a lovely gift for someone who enjoys making cocktails. Use your home dried ingredients, or buy from health or international food shops.

Use your favourite cocktail recipes or experiment with your own combinations using the dried herb, fruit and edible flowers suggestions in this book (or search the web for other mixology ideas).

Some flowers will add a subtle colour too: calendula for a light orange-yellow, cornflower for a light blue or blue butterfly pea flower for a deep lapis lazuli.

The recipe here is for half a litre of spirits (approximately 1 pint): gin, vodka, tequila, rum, whisky, bourbon or brandy.

YOU WILL NEED

A clean wide mouthed bottle or jar with a lid, big enough for the herbs and the liquid

3 tbsp dried herbs, flowers and/or fruit

500ml (17½fl.oz) spirits

Pour your combination into the bottle. Attach a label with instructions, for example:

To make the infusion, fill the bottle with your chosen spirits and shake daily for one week before tasting. For a stronger flavour leave to infuse for up to three more weeks, tasting weekly.

Strain, discard the herbs and return to the bottle. Enjoy!

SOME COMBINATION IDEAS

Rose geranium and raspberry

Lavender and dried lemon peel

Rose petals, lemon verbena and borage

Lemongrass, lime peel and blue butterfly pea flower

Lavender and rosemary

Strawberry, mint and rose petals

Lemongrass, chilli and coriander seeds

Strawberry and rosemary

Mint and dried orange peel

Basil and lemon balm

Mint and lemon verbena

Chamomile and cornflower

6
CRAFTS

You have made your meals; your shelves contain infusing brews and jars of homemade seasonings, liqueurs and tea blends. If you are like me, you'll start thinking: "What else can I make?"

Here are some suggestions for 'beyond the dinner table' uses for vegetables, herbs and foraged plants. These are great activities to do with children, friends or community groups. Some are practical solutions for the home, others make lovely treats for yourself or gifts to share.

Only use containers that you are certain are heat-proof for anything which involves pouring in hot liquids.

Beetroot lip gloss

This recipe uses dehydrated beetroot powder. The dehydrated beetroot slices make a tasty snack (I like them with a sprinkle of seasoned salt or a splash of tamari) and the powder can also be used in cooking, to add a natural pink colour to baking, sauces and soups. Store the dried slices and powder in glass jars in a cool, dark place.

All colours of beetroot make tasty snacks dehydrated and can also be powdered for culinary uses.

How to make dehydrated beetroot powder

Red beetroot (for a pink/red colour)

(The quantity depends how large your dehydrator is. If you are not sure, peel and slice one beetroot at a time, then layer in the dehydrator until it is full)

A dehydrator (you can use an oven if you don't have one)

A food processor or coffee/nut grinder

Wear something to protect your clothes! Red beetroot stains enthusiastically

Peel the beetroot and cut into 2mm slices carefully with a sharp kitchen knife. You could also use a mandolin or slice attachment on a food processor.

This will stain your hands red! If this is a concern, you could wear food grade gloves. Alternatively, scrub your hands with lemon juice or lemon hand scrub, wash thoroughly and dry. The staining doesn't bother me and it is usually gone within a few hours.

Layer the beetroot on the dehydrator. Follow the directions for your machine and dehydrate until the beetroot slices are dry and crisp. Reserve any that you are saving as a snack.

If you do not have a dehydrator, the beetroot can be dried instead in a low oven. Spread the sliced beetroot in single layers on baking trays and put in the oven at the lowest setting for around four hours. How long this will take depends on your oven, so check every hour.

Place dried beetroot slices in the food processor and grind to make a fine powder. Do not over fill your food processor or grinder – you may need to repeat this several times, depending how much beetroot you have dehydrated.

TIP   If you have extra space in your dehydrator or oven, chop and spread the beetroot greens to dehydrate. They will take much less time than the beetroot so check regularly until they feel dry and crispy. These are so delicious as a snack or sprinkled on food and keep for months stored in a glass jar.

TIP   The beetroot powder makes a lovely light blusher applied with a brush. For a lighter hue, experiment with mixing red beetroot and pink Chioggia beetroot powders.

How to make beetroot lip gloss

2-3 tsp beetroot powder
(less for a lighter colour, more for a
deeper gloss)

2 tsp almond oil

2 tsp coconut oil

2 tsp shea butter

Small containers*

Place the almond oil, coconut oil and shea butter in a heatproof bowl over a pan of boiling water (a bain marie) and stir until melted and combined. Remove from the pan and stir in the beetroot powder. Mix thoroughly.

Pour the liquid into your containers and allow to cool.

This versatile lip gloss can also be used as a blusher.

* You can reuse thoroughly washed lip salve tins or tubes, or tiny glass jam jars, or buy new ones from soap and cosmetic suppliers. 100% biodegradable cardboard lip gloss tubes are available to buy online, but at the time of writing are only available in the UK bought in bulk (or very expensively in smaller quantities).

Beetroot tinted lip gloss without using a dehydrator

Peel and chop one beetroot, put in a food processor and blend into a purée. Do not add water. You want the intense colour of whole beetroot juice.

Pour into a sieve over a jug, place a saucer with a weight on top of the beetroot purée (this helps all of the juice to ooze through) and allow the juice to drip into the jug. (Alternatively you can use a juicer.) Pour into a clean lidded jar.

Toss the beetroot residue into the compost or add to soups, pâtés, etc. or freeze in an ice cube tray for later use as an addition to soups, sauces, etc.

TO MAKE THE LIP GLOSS

2 tsp beetroot juice

1 tsp cocoa butter

1 tsp shea butter

1 tbsp coconut oil (or almond oil)

2 tsp soy or beeswax (1 tsp candelilla wax)

Place all of the ingredients except the beetroot juice in a heatproof bowl and put over a pan of boiling water. Stir until everything has melted and combined. Remove from the pan.

Slowly add the beetroot juice, stirring continually, until thoroughly mixed.

Pour into containers (as for the recipe above) and leave to cool.

Infused oil lip balm

This recipe uses your own choice of infused oil (see page 27) to make a clear lip balm which is ideal for everyone.

Suggested infused oils to use: lavender, calendula, lemon verbena, mint, lemon balm.

6 tsp infused oil – coconut, almond oil, olive oil

6 tsp cocoa butter

3 tsp soy or beeswax (1½ tsp candelilla wax)

Place the ingredients in a heatproof dish over a pan of boiling water and stir continually until dissolved. Remove from the heat and pour into your containers. Leave to cool.

Homegrown face masks

Revive your skin with these freshly prepared face masks. As you won't be eating them, you can use fruit and vegetables which have been nibbled and might otherwise have been discarded. After use, the face masks can be composted.

I blend oats in a coffee grinder to make oatmeal. You can omit the oatmeal, but it does help to make the mixture less liquid.

To make these masks, simply mix the ingredients together and apply to the face. Avoid contact with the eye area. Lie down and relax for 10 minutes, then wipe off and wash.

These can be a bit drippy, so take care with clothes and your surroundings. Best to protect any soft furnishings with a towel.

Carrot face mask

2 carrots, blended with a splash of water into a purée

2 tbsp oatmeal

Parsley and cucumber face mask

½ cucumber

1 tbsp chopped parsley

Blend together in a food processor

Raspberry or strawberry face mask

½ cup fruit, mashed

2 tbsp oatmeal

Pumpkin/squash face mask

4 tbsp pumpkin or squash purée (cooked or raw)

2 tbsp oatmeal

rose petal
bath scrub

Tomato and cucumber face mask

1 tomato

¼ cucumber

Blend together. Add 2 tsp oatmeal if it is too liquid.

Pumpkin body scrub

This spicy scrub revives the skin and smells of pumpkin pie.

60ml (2fl.oz/¼ cup) pumpkin or squash purée

200g (7oz/1 cup) sugar

2 tsp mixed spice

Mix together in a bowl. This will keep for three days in the fridge.

Rose petal bath scrub

14g (½oz/1 cup) rose petals

400g (14oz/2 cups) sugar

160ml (5½fl.oz/⅔ cup) infused olive oil (e.g. rose petal oil, calendula, chamomile – use a light fragranced oil to allow the scent of the rose petals to come through)

Put the rose petals in a food processor and grind into small flakes (this is to prevent the plug hole from being blocked).

Put in a bowl with the sugar and oil. Mix together until fully combined. Put into glass jars, label and decorate, if you wish.

NOTE   I always use unbleached organic sugar in my body scrubs. This makes them slightly darker than refined sugar. You can use any sugar in these recipes.

Rosemary hair rinse

950ml (33½fl.oz/4 cups) water

4 tbsp fresh rosemary (or 2 tbsp dried rosemary)

Put the rosemary and water in a pan, bring to the boil and simmer for 30 minutes. Leave to cool with the lid on.

When cool, strain and pour into a glass bottle.

Use as a stimulating final rinse when washing hair. The rosemary is said to encourage hair growth and stimulates the scalp.

toothpowder

toothpaste

Homemade toothpowder

I first came across the idea of using a powdered clay based toothpowder when I met a woman selling it at the Offgrid Festival three or four years ago. Until then, I had been using a fluoride free toothpaste from the local whole food shop (no artificial sweeteners, SLS etc.) which was fine – however trying this was a revelation! It made my teeth feel really clean and felt so much healthier and pleasanter in my mouth than toothpaste. It lasts a long time, is cheap to make and easy to store. This toothpowder keeps my teeth clean, helps to remove toxins and also can help (according to what I have read) remineralise my teeth.

Bentonite clay naturally detoxes and can help eliminate toxins, and it is also full of minerals which are beneficial for gums and teeth.

Bicarbonate of soda, which gently whitens and polishes teeth, is an ingredient found in many commercial brands of toothpaste too.

Sea salt is also rich in minerals, removes tartar, whitens teeth and is beneficial for oral hygiene. I make a sea salt mouth wash sometimes, a teaspoon dissolved in warm water, a technique recommended by a dentist.

YOU WILL NEED

1 tbsp of sea salt, finely ground –
I grind salt crystals in a herb grinder

4 tbsp bentonite clay

4 tbsp bicarbonate of soda

A glass jar

Put everything in the glass jar and replace the lid.

Shake it to mix well!

And there you are – a jar of toothpowder. If you like, you can add some finely ground dried mint, sage, fennel or lemon balm for flavour but I like it just like this. I keep a small jar of this in my bathroom cabinet, refilling it from the larger jar when needed. This helps to keep the powder dry and fresh.

To use, just dip your toothbrush in the powder and brush and rinse as normal.

Homemade toothpaste

If you prefer something creamier.

½ cup homemade toothpowder

½ cup coconut oil

Finely ground herbs or spices (as above) (optional)

Mix together thoroughly and store in a labelled jar. To use, place a pea sized amount on your toothbrush.

Gardeners' hand scrub

This hand scrub is handy to have by the sink. It smells lovely and scrubs away dirt and grime. Condition your hands after rubbing with some of the gardeners hand salve.

Unbleached sugar

Dried herbs e.g. rosemary, lavender, mint, lemon balm, lemon verbena, thyme, parsley

Ground aduki beans or almonds (optional)

Liquid castile soap, liquid hand wash or washing up liquid

Fill a clean jar to about ¾ with sugar (or a mixture of 50/50 sugar and aduki beans or almonds, ground in a nut grinder for extra cleansing power).

Add 1 tsp of dried herbs.

Pour washing up liquid in, almost to the top. Stir with a spoon. Replace the lid and label the jar.

Use with warm water to clean and soften the hands.

Gardeners' hand salve

236ml (8¼fl.oz/1 cup) olive oil

1 tbsp calendula petals

1 tbsp scented rose pelargonium flowers and leaves

1 tbsp lemon balm

5 tbsp candelilla or soy wax

A large jar with a lid

Containers with lids for pouring the salve into

TIP You can use any herbs and flowers you like in this recipe.

Infuse the oil with the herbs and flowers by placing in a jar, lightly crushing and pouring over the oil and allowing to infuse for two weeks. Strain through muslin and pour into a labelled jar until you are ready to make the salve.

In a bain marie, melt the infused oil and candelilla wax together, stirring all of the time.

Remove from the heat and pour into the containers. Label.

I like to have a small jam jar beside the sink and use small metal tins to keep in my gardening trug or for taking travelling.

Soap made from scraps of soap

We keep a dish in the airing cupboard for odds and ends of soap scraps, ready to be melted into new bars.

Saved slivers of soap

1 tbsp oatmeal per cup of soap
(if you don't have oatmeal, grind some oats in a food processor)
or 1 tbsp coffee grounds

1 tsp ground dried herbs per cup of soap
(e.g. mint, lemon verbena, rosemary)

Dried flower petals to decorate

Water (infused with herbs if you wish, and strained)

A glass bowl and pan, or a double boiler
(a bain marie)

Soap moulds – use items from around the house: e.g. muffin tins, small food tins

Grate or finely chop the soap.

Measure the grated soap into the glass bowl. For each cup of flakes, add ¼ cup water.

Place over a pan of simmering water to melt, stirring continually. You may need to add more water to help it all melt. The amount of water needed depends on the type of soaps you are melting, so add the extra water a little at a time until it is thick and creamy.

Any small lumps that are refusing to melt do not matter, they just add to the charm of a homemade soap.

Once the soap is melted, remove from the heat and stir in the oatmeal and dried herbs.

Stir to thoroughly combine and pour into your moulds.

Gently press on dried flowers, petals and herbs if you wish.

Leave to dry for 24 hours before removing from the moulds.

Beard oil

Beard oil helps to keep the beard and skin in good condition. It cleanses and moisturises, reducing dryness and helping to keep the natural balance of the body's oils. Used with a beard comb, the beard oil keeps the beard clean and tangle-free.

Use your choice of infused oils to make this grooming oil.

Good oils to use: argan, jojoba, olive, grapeseed, rosehip, coconut, almond

Addition – Vitamin E. I usually buy capsules and add the contents of one to the blend

DELICIOUS BEARD OIL COMBINATIONS:

Lime and rosemary

Mint and lavender

Calendula and rose

Orange, lemon and lime

Sage, thyme and rosemary

Basil and lemon verbena

'Beard Mojito' – lime and mint

Choose two oils and infuse separately (or combine first and infuse) with your choice of lime, orange or lemon peel, rosemary, basil (flower or leaf), lavender, rose, calendula, sage, mint, thyme, lemon verbena, lemongrass (see page 25).

Mix the two oils together (if not already combined). For each 136ml (4½fl.oz/½ cup) oil add the contents of one vitamin E capsule. Shake to mix.

Pour into a dark labelled bottle with a dropper.

To use: depending on the length of the beard, drip 3-6 drops of beard oil into the palm of the hand. Rub hands together and apply to the beard, massaging into the hair and skin. Comb with a beard comb, if desired.

Tussie mussie

A Tussie Mussie is a small bouquet which became fashionable in Victorian times but has existed as a floral accessory since Mediaeval times. Also known as a Nose-gay, Tussie Mussies were often given as gifts and were held or worn attached to clothes.

This would be a delightful addition to a gift basket of homemade cosmetics and bath potions.

I've been using bunches of herbs in the bath for years, but came across the idea of calling them by this old fashioned name when visiting Babylonstoren in South Africa. There, guests are offered a tightly fastened bundle of herbs and scented flowers grown in their expansive gardens, to fragrance their bath.

When running the bath, add the Tussie Mussie to the water to release the fragrant herbal oils from the plants. You can also use it as a gentle body exfoliator.

The Tussie Mussie can be reused for about three days, just hang on the taps to dry out after use. Be sure to use natural twine to fasten the Tussie Mussie together, so that it can easily be composted.

How to make your tussie mussie

A selection of herbs, cut into 8in lengths

Natural, biodegradable string to fasten

Gather your herbs on a dry day, shaking to dislodge any lurking insects. Holding them in a bundle, tightly wrap the string around the stems creating a lovely bunch. Leave enough string to make a loop for hanging when drying out, if you wish.

Suggested herbs to use: scented pelargoniums, lemon verbena, thyme, rosemary, lavender, sage, lemongrass, yarrow, chamomile.

Herbal bath and shower teas

You can use fresh or dried herbs to make these bath teas. Choose herbs to reflect the effect you wish to have – relaxing herbs at bedtime, invigorating herbs in the morning.

Reusable herb infuser balls are widely available to buy; these are only for baths rather than showers. Alternatively, make your own bathroom herbal tea bags.

YOU WILL NEED

Old cotton fabric (shirt, t-shirt, etc.) or cheese cloth/muslin

A plate 22cm/8.7in diameter (approx. larger is fine too)

Thick sewing thread (to make a draw string) and a needle

Soft pencil

VARIATIONS

Suggested contents:
chamomile, sage, lavender, lemon balm, lemon verbena, rose petals, thyme, calendula, green tea, oats, dried citrus peels

Relaxing bedtime blend:
chamomile and calendula

Perk up blend (great for reviving the brain and body when studying):
rosemary, lemon balm and sage

Skin soothing blend:
chamomile and oats

Calming blend:
rose petals, green tea and lavender

Invigorating blend:
mint, lemongrass and citrus peels

Using the plate as a template, cut circles of cloth.

Measure 6cm/2.4in from the edge of the cloth and draw a circle (make sure the 'good' side of the fabric is facing downwards).

With the 'good' side of the fabric facing downwards and leaving 12cm/5in of thread on the outside, push the needle from behind and using a running stitch, sow around the circle you have drawn. Make sure that the ends of the thread are both on the 'good' side of the fabric.

Tie the two ends together.

To make your bathroom tea bags, place 2 tbsp of herbs into the centre of the 'tea bag' as shown and pull the drawstring together to make a little bag.

Hang over the hot tap when running the bath to infuse with the herbs. You can also scrub the skin with this bag in the bath or shower.

Reuse two or three times, before discarding the contents in the compost heap. The 'tea bags' can be washed over and reused many times.

For an 'instant tea bag', stuff the toe of an old odd sock or stocking with herbs and tie with string. Or use a handkerchief or similar piece of fabric, tied with an elastic band or string.

Herbal floral natural bath bombs

Containing nourishing oils and salts, these bath bombs are wonderful for relaxing bath times and are lovely use for your homegrown herbs, flowers and infused oils. Added to the water, the delightful fizzing releases herbs and flowers, for a sensuous cleansing bath.

They make thoughtful, gorgeous gifts.

YOU WILL NEED

225g (8oz/1 cup) bicarbonate of soda (baking soda)

115g (4oz/½ cup) citric acid

115g (4oz/½ cup) salt*

2 tbsp infused oil of your choice

Dried crumbled herbs

Dried flower petals

Witch hazel in a small spray bottle
A bowl and spoon

*   use one or a combination of Epsom salt, sea salt, rock salt or Dead Sea salt

MOULDS

Muffin tins: silicone is especially good for bath bombs as they are easier to remove. If you are using metal tins, line with some recycled polythene (the thick plastic that nuts and pulses come in is useful for this) or muffin cases

2 piece round bath bomb moulds; these come in a variety of sizes

Household items including soap or chocolate moulds, ice cube trays, cookie cutters

TIP   If you have cuts or sensitive skin, wear gloves to make the bath bombs.

Put the bicarbonate of soda, citric acid and salt into a bowl and mix together with a spoon.

Pour the oil into the mix and stir to combine.

Add a few squirts of witch hazel and stir. Squeeze with your hand; it should clump together. If it is not ready, add more witch hazel until it clumps.

Sprinkle some flowers and herbs on the bottom of your moulds. Spoon some mixture into the mould and press down with the back of the spoon to cover the bottom.

Next, sprinkle a layer of herbs and flowers, add more mixture and so on until the mould is full. Decorate with more herbs or flowers and press into place with the back of the spoon or your fingers.

Leave to harden for 24 hours.

Remove from the moulds and store in airtight containers until use. The bath bombs are ready to use now if you can't wait to try one out.

Hair brush cleaning kit

Revive your hairbrush with these gentle, effective cleaning potions

Hair brush spray

236ml (8fl.oz/1 cup) rosemary infused vinegar (or infused vinegar of your choice)

236ml (8fl.oz/1 cup) water

Mix together and pour into a labelled spray bottle.

Hair brush powder

245g (8½oz/1 cup) baking soda

25g (1oz/½ cup) dried herbs, finely ground (choose from rosemary, mint, lemon balm, scented pelargonium, thyme)

Mix together and store in a labelled jar.

Clean your hairbrush, using tweezers, a toothpick or similar shaped implement to remove all traces of hair and fluff. An old toothbrush can be an effective debris remover too.

Sprinkle the bristles with the hair brush powder. Use an old toothbrush make sure the bristle area is thoroughly coated. Leave for 30 minutes and then remove with a clean old toothbrush.

Next, spray with the hair brush spray. Use a soft cloth or old toothbrush to make sure the bristles are thoroughly cleaned. Put in a sunny place to dry.

This will help keep your hair clean and prolong the life of your hairbrush.

Natural insect repelling tussie mussie

Hang bunches of herbs around your home to help deter flies and other unwanted insects. They smell and look gorgeous too.

Plants with insect repelling properties include:

Lemon scented pelargoniums

Lavender

Lemongrass

Lemon thyme

Rosemary

Dill

Tansy

Pennyroyal

Wormwood

Sweet woodruff

Gather bunches of the herbs and tie together tightly, leaving enough string to make a loop for hanging.

insect repelling
tussie mussie

Herbal fizzy toilet bombs

These fizzy toilet bombs help to keep your loo fresh and clean and also reduce limescale residue in the bowl. Store in an airtight glass jar in your bathroom.

To use, pop one into the toilet bowl. When it has finished fizzing, finish with some citrus or herb cleaning vinegar and scrub with a toilet brush, before flushing.

240g (8½oz/2 cups) citric acid

160g (5½oz/⅔ cup) baking soda

2 tsp water in a small spray bottle (use herbal infused water if you have some)

3 tsp dried herbs or citrus peels, ground into a powder

Small moulds, for example ice cube trays or small soap moulds

Pour the citric acid, baking soda and 2 tsp of ground herbs or peels into a bowl and stir with a spoon to combine.

Add the water, spraying a little at a time, combining with your hands until the mixture holds its shape when squeezed together (wear gloves if your hands are sensitive).

Sprinkle the rest of the herbs into the bottom of the moulds. Fill with the mixture and press down with the back of a spoon or your fingers. Leave to dry for 24 hours.

Pop out of the moulds and store in airtight containers.

Herbal or citrus cleaning vinegar

This recipe, also in *No Dig Organic Home and Garden*, makes an effective toilet cleaner which works well with the toilet bombs.

Loosely fill a glass jar ¾ full with herbs (e.g. rosemary, lemon verbena, thyme, scented pelargonium) or citrus peels. Fill to the top with white vinegar (or cider vinegar), replace the lid and leave for two weeks.

Strain through a sieve into a clean labelled jar or bottle.

Use neat in the toilet bowl or mix 50/50 with water in a spray bottle for an effective toilet spray cleaner.

Herb candles

This makes enough for four 8oz candles, depending on the size of your jars.

YOU WILL NEED

FOR THE PRESSED HERBS AND FLOWERS

Herbs and flowers of your choice

A flower press or some heavy books and thick clean paper

FOR THE CANDLES

Glass jars suitable for candles – I reuse old candle jars or solid preserving jars

Wicks and metal bases, enough for the jars

8 cups soy wax
(or grated odds and ends from old candles)

25 drops essential oil
(your choice of fragrance, choose one which compliments your dried herbs)

2 tsp dried herbs, finely ground

A clean tin can or glass bowl for melting the wax

A pan ⅓ full of water – to make a bain marie

Pencils or clothes pins
(the wooden kind which clip)

Skewers

Brush

Tongs

Tea towels, one for each jar

Layer your herbs and flowers in the flower press, or put between sheets of thick, clean paper and place several very heavy books on top.

Leave for a week until dry and very flat.

Bring the water to the boil and reduce to a simmer. Place the tin or bowl of wax over the pan and melt the wax, stirring often. This should take about five minutes. Turn off the heat but leave the wax over the water to remain melted. Stir in the essential oil and ground herbs.

Using the skewer, drip some wax at the bottom of the jars to fix the wick metal plates. Dip the ends of the wicks in the melted wax and using the skewer to help fix it in, place the wick in the metal base and hold with the skewer until fixed. Use the pencils or clothes pins to hold the wick in place.

Dip the pressed herbs carefully into the wax using the tongs. Press against the side of the jars, holding in place with a skewer until the wax has dried before adding the next decoration.

Brush the dried herbs with melted wax to keep them in place when the melted wax is poured in. Carefully pour the wax into the jars.

Wrap each jar in a tea towel. This helps to slow down the cooling process which makes a better candle. Leave the candles for 48 hours to cool thoroughly. Remove the clothes pins or pencils and trim the wick to 2.5cm.

As with all candles, never leave a burning flame unattended and keep out of the reach of children and pets. Make sure the herbs are not placed close to the wick to ensure that they do not ignite.

Boot and shoe balm

This boot balm works on all kinds of waterproof boots and shoes but do check a small area first.

200ml (7fl.oz/¾ cup) infused olive oil
(any fragrance you like)

50g (1½oz) soy wax or beeswax

Place in a heatproof dish over a pan of boiling water. Reduce the heat to a simmer and dissolve the wax in the oil stirring continually.

Remove from the heat and pour into a heat resistant jar. Allow to cool, then replace the lid and label.

To use, apply with a cloth or boot brush and rub all over. Buff with a clean, soft cloth.

Herbal footwear pot pourri bags

These bags deodorise and also help to reduce moisture in shoes and boots. Make different sizes according to the footwear. I use smaller ones in trainers and stuff old socks for my wellies. It's a great way of making use of lonely odd socks and is especially useful for seasonal footwear which is being stored for a few months.

YOU WILL NEED

Odd socks, all shapes and sizes or tights/pantyhose
or
Circles of cloth cut from old t-shirts, shirts, etc. Use a plate as a template (see page 192)

Scraps of cloth for stuffing (if needed)

String, ribbon or elastic bands

Dried herbs and flowers –
experiment with your choice of fragrant dried herbs and flowers to get the right mix for your feet, for example rosemary, scented pelargonium, sage, thyme, mint, lemon balm, lemon verbena, eucalyptus, chamomile

Bicarbonate of soda

Arrowroot

TIP These bags are also useful fresheners in wardrobes, cupboards and drawers.

The quantities will vary according to the size of your homemade bag or sock, but the ratio of bicarbonate of soda to arrowroot remains the same, 1:1. So if you use one cup of arrowroot, mix it with one cup of bicarbonate of soda. This mixture helps to absorb moisture and deodorise, keeping footwear fresh and lasting longer.

To make pot pourri footwear bags, first cut circles the size you want for the shoes out of your cloth – two of the same size for each pair of footwear.

You can use any kind of cup as you measure, a measuring cup, tea cup, mug, etc. Just keep the ratios the same.

Mix 1 cup of bicarbonate of soda/arrowroot mix with 3 cups of dried herbs and flowers in a large bowl. This will be enough for several bags. Make according to your needs.

Scoop 1 cup of this mixture into the centre of each cloth circle (½ cup if its a small bag for children's shoes). Gather up the circle and fasten using string, ribbon or an elastic band. Repeat to make a second bag.

To use, slide the bags into the shoes.

To make pot pourri deodorising socks find two similar sized odd socks for each pair of shoes or boots. Make up the pot pourri mixture as described above and pour a cup (two or more for wellies) into the 'foot' of the sock. Using scraps of fabric (or more pot pourri mixture if you prefer) loosely stuff the sock until it resembles a foot. Fasten tightly at the top with string or an elastic band. Stuff into your shoes or boots to freshen and deodorise.

To freshen up the deodorising bags, hang in a dry airy place for 24 hours.

Cleaning wooden chopping boards

I much prefer to use wooden or bamboo chopping boards rather than plastic. They are hard wearing, easy to clean, long lasting, kind to my knives and if they eventually do break, can be easily upcycled into something else or used as firewood. It is important to keep your chopping boards clean, whichever you prefer to use. These recipes are designed for wooden and bamboo boards, but the scrubs and sprays will also work well on plastic (don't use the oil on plastic boards though!).

In addition to these recipes you will need hot water, cleaning cloths and a scrubbing brush. A small wooden scraper can be useful too.

These recipes are ideal for unvarnished wooden kitchen tables – don't use on anything fancy!

Simple lemon and salt scrub

Coarse grain salt

1 lemon, cut in half

Wash your board to remove any crumbs, dirt etc.

Sprinkle with the salt and use half a lemon to scrub. This will help to sanitise and remove stains.

If you are cleaning a lot of wood, you may need to use more salt and the other half lemon. Use a scrubbing brush or scraper to remove anything stubborn.

Put the lemon in the compost and leave the salty boards for 30 minutes, then wash with warm water and allow to dry.

lemon and salt paste

zingy kitchen and wooden board scrub

Lemon and salt paste

This is useful for awkward shaped areas or to use up spare lemon juice.

120g (4oz/½ cup) coarse salt

½ lemon, juice

Old toothbrush and soft cloths or a scrubbing brush

Mix together the salt and lemon juice and apply using a cloth or scrubbing brush, using a toothbrush for any awkward to reach areas. Continue as for the Simple lemon and salt scrub.

Zingy kitchen and wooden board scrub

2 tbsp dried ground zest from lemons, oranges or limes

2 tbsp dried ground lemon balm or lemon verbena

1 cup coarse salt

Mix the ingredients together and store in a labelled jar.

Use as above, but apply with a damp brush or cloth. This scrub is also good for cleaning taps, sinks, work surfaces and bathrooms.

cider vinegar spray

Cider vinegar herbal spray

236ml (8fl.oz/1 cup) water

236ml (8fl.oz/1 cup) rosemary, lemon balm and mint infused cider vinegar (see page 25)

Mix together and pour into a labelled spray bottle.

Spray boards, surfaces, taps and sinks after scrubbing with a salt scrub. Wipe with a damp cloth and polish to a shine (for taps and other shining surfaces). This spray is a good, all round household spray – ideal for bathrooms and windows too.

Conditioning oil for wooden utensils

236ml (8fl.oz/1 cup) walnut oil

60g (2oz/½ cup) soy or other plant based wax

ALTERNATIVES

Use olive, sunflower, grape seed or other light oil in place of the walnut, as it is or infused with citrus peels, mint, rosemary, lemon balm or thyme. These oils can become rancid after time, unlike walnut oil, but in a kitchen environment where tools are regularly used and washed, I have not found myself that this has ever been a problem.

Put the walnut oil and wax in a heatproof dish and place over a pan of boiling water. Reducing the heat to a simmer, melt the wax and oil together, stirring continually.

Pour carefully into a heatproof lidded jar, one that you would use for canning will be fine, e.g. Weck, Kilner, Bell.

When cool, apply to your wooden utensils, boards, tables and other indoor wooden items. This oil is food grade but of course should not be used by anyone allergic to walnuts or soy (if using soy wax).

Outdoor wood oil

115ml (4fl.oz/½ cup) linseed oil

115ml (4fl.oz/½ cup) infused grape seed or sunflower oil (rosemary, thyme, lemon balm, sage, mint)

60g (2oz/½ cup) soy wax or beeswax

Make as the oil for wooden utensils.

To apply, sandpaper the area to be treated (if necessary) and scrub. When dry, apply the oil with a brush or soft cloth.

This oil is great to use on wooden handled garden equipment.

conditioning oil

for wooden utensils

Rose pelargonium infused wood oil

This oil is lovely for conditioning wooden furniture and other wooden items in the home. The leaves of rose scented pelargoniums have been used for centuries crushed and rubbed onto wood to condition it. This oil harnesses the nurturing power of this deliciously fragranced herb in an easier to apply conditioning oil.

1 large jar with a lid

1 part fresh rose pelargonium flowers and leaves

2 parts olive or walnut oil

Vinegar (cider or white) or lemon juice

Place the flowers and leaves in the jar, crushing gently as you do so. Fill to about $1/3$. Pour over the olive oil and replace the lid.

Leave in a cool place out of direct sunlight for two weeks, shaking every day. Make sure the leaves remain under the oil whilst it is infusing. Use a fermenting weight or similar to hold them under if necessary.

Strain through a muslin lined colander and pour into another clean jar. Label 'Rose pelargonium oil'.

To make the wood oil, mix 3 parts infused oil with 1 part lemon juice or vinegar, in a clean lidded jar, e.g. 75ml oil to 25ml vinegar or lemon juice.

Shake to combine.

Apply to the wood with a clean cloth and buff to a shine.

TIP Sweet cicely leaves and green seed pods make an excellent wood oil too. Infuse as the rose pelargonium.

APPENDIX:
BEANS, TOMATOES AND OTHER INGREDIENTS

Recognising that it is sometimes not humanly possible to use entirely fresh ingredients, as far as possible the quantities for cooked pulses and tomatoes in this book are the equivalent of a 400g (14oz) can. I always have some in the cupboard, ideal for quickly making a meal at the end of a busy day.

A 400g (14oz) can of pulses has a drained weight of approximately 240g (8½oz).

How to cook dried beans – two ways

All beans and other pulses will vary slightly depending on age and variety, but generally they triple in weight after cooking.

I usually soak and cook far more than I need so that I can store some in the freezer for another day.

Overnight soaking

Measure the beans into a large container and pour over enough water to cover with at least 5cm/2in water. Leave overnight to soak.

Quick soaking

This is very handy if you forget to put the beans to soak before you go to bed! Put the beans and water into a large pan, cover with at least 5cm/2in water, bring to the boil and cook for 10 minutes. Turn off the heat and leave to soak for two hours. Drain and cook.

Cooking

Drain and place in a large pan and add enough water to cover with at least 5cm/2in water. Add herbs (e.g. bay leaf, rosemary, thyme), a sliced onion or garlic if wished and bring to the boil. Reduce the heat and simmer, stirring occasionally.

The cooking time depends on the pulses, usually around 30-40 minutes, less for lentils.

The beans are ready when they are soft but still have their shape (not mushy!). I check by fishing one out with a slotted spoon occasionally, letting it cool a bit and seeing if it is cooked.

Cooking in a slow cooker

A slow cooker takes much longer, but has the advantage that you can set the timer and go off to do other things.

Add the beans, boiling water and aromatic herbs, onions or garlic to the pan as above, boil for 10 minutes and carefully pour into the slow cooker, covering with at least 5cm/2in water. I use a small jug for this; much safer than pouring from the pan. Bring to the boil then reduce to the low setting and set the timer (if there is one) for 4-6 hours.

The cooking liquid

The cooking liquid is tasty! Use as you would vegetable stock, it freezes well for about six months.

I don't use the liquid from cans of beans, except chickpeas.

RESOURCES

No Dig Organic Home and Garden
Charles Dowding and Stephanie Hafferty, Permanent Publications, 2017.

Winner of the Peter Seabrook Practical Book of the Year Award 2017, this book combines the practical growing experience of Charles and Stephanie and also includes many recipes for the kitchen, home and garden. If you want to learn how to create a productive no dig garden, this is the book for you.

www.nodighome.com
No Dig Home is Stephanie's blog which includes lots of recipes and posts about her gardening adventures, making potions and small scale homesteading in her garden and allotment.

www.stephaniehafferty.co.uk
Information on Stephanie's workshops, courses and talks.

www.charlesdowding.co.uk
A wealth of information on no dig, seasonal updates on vegetable growing and Charles, many workshops, talks and courses (Stephanie cooks her seasonal meals for the courses at Homeacres).

SUPPLIERS

Hodmedods
www.hodmedods.co.uk
For a wide range of UK grown pulses and flours, including flours made from peas and quinoa. Buy online or email them for a list of stores they supply near you. Their website includes recipes.

Naturally Balmy
www.naturallybalmy.co.uk
For a wide range of vegan waxes, beeswax, plant butters, oils and other ingredients for making skin care.

The Soap Kitchen
www.thesoapkitchen.co.uk
A good range of products for making soaps, bath bombs and other toiletries, including small metal tins for lip balms.

Weck
www.weckjars.com
Many of the glass jars featured in this book are made by Weck. I use them because I also have a Weck water bath canner. Weck jars come in a beautiful range of shapes and sizes. The glass lids with metal fasteners make them a plastic free option and they are freezer safe.

INDEX

Enjoyed this book?
You might like these

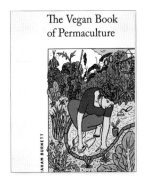

Get 15% off any of our other books above with
discount code: **CREATIVE**
Just visit: https://shop.permaculture.co.uk

Our titles cover: permaculture, home & garden, green
building, food & drink, sustainable technology,
woodlands, community, wellbeing and so much more

See our full range of books here:

www.permanentpublications.co.uk

Subscribe to a better world

Each issue of *Permaculture Magazine International* is hand crafted, sharing practical, innovative solutions, money saving ideas and global perspectives from a grassroots movement in over 170 countries

Print subscribers receive FREE digital access to our complete 26 years of back issues plus bonus content

To subscribe call 01730 823 311 or visit:

www.permaculture.co.uk